Images 33 /
Best of British
Illustration 2009

ΛOI
Association
of illustrators

Images 33

Edited and published by
The Association of Illustrators
2nd Floor, Back Building
150 Curtain Road
London EC2A 3AT
Tel. +44 (0)20 7613 4328
Fax +44 (0)20 7613 4417
info@theaoi.com
theAOI.com
AOIimages.com

ISBN 978-0-9558076-8-8
Production in Hong Kong by
Hong Kong Graphics and Printing Ltd
Tel: (852) 2976 0289
Fax: (852) 2976 0292

Art Director /
Adrian Shaughnessy
shaughnessyworks.com

Design & Artwork /
Simon Sharville
simonsharville.co.uk

Portrait illustrations /
Hannah Buck
hannah-buck.com

The Association of Illustrators

AOI Board of Directors /
Beach, Russell Cobb, Andrew Coningsby, Adam Graff (up to Spring 2009), Annabel Hudson (from Spring 2009), Rod Hunt, Simon Pemberton

AOI Chair /
Russell Cobb

AOI Deputy Chair /
Rod Hunt

AOI Images Committee /
Ramón Blomfield, Derek Brazell, Jareh Das, Adam Graff, Rod Hunt, Sabine Reimer

Advisers /
Stephanie Alexander, Alison Branagan, Ruth Gladwin, Tony Healey, Matt Johnson, Christine Jopling, Robert Lands, Alison Lang, Samantha Lewis, Simon Stern, Fig Taylor, Anna Vernon, Bee Willey, Jo Young

Managing Director /
Ramón Blomfield (from November 08)
ramon@theaoi.com

Special Projects Manager /
Derek Brazell
derek@theaoi.com

Images Co-ordinator /
Sabine Reimer
images@theaoi.com

Marketing and Events Co-ordinator /
Jareh Das
events@theaoi.com

Membership Co-ordinators /
Becky Brown and Nicolette Hamilton
info@theaoi.com

Finance Officer /
Ian Veacock BA(Hons) FCCA
finance@theaoi.com

i33 / Contents

i33 / Contents

In spite of a tough year in the economy, Images 2009 positively glows with optimism. It looks better than ever.

First of all there's the book itself. This year Adrian Shaughnessy, acclaimed art director, writer and design consultant, is our guest art director. After bringing much industry acclaim and awards to Varoom magazine, Adrian has cast his keen eye onto Images and provided us with something bold and instantly collectable. Everyone interested in the best of British illustration will want to look at it, run their hands over it, and keep it on a reachable shelf. A very big and grateful thank-you to him for his hard work and inspiration.

Then there are the contents themselves. Once again, the work is of the very highest standard. Diverse. Inventive. Brilliant. In world terms, British illustration is still a world leader. Congratulations to all this year's winners and selected artists.

Let's not forget, too, that Images is the only UK jury-selected awards book for illustration. In other words it's both a source book and an awards annual. And in these difficult times, commissioning people are looking for the value for money that impactful, award-winning illustrators can give them. Many are choosing original illustration as a more viable choice over photography. Where better to search for it than Images 2009?

So.

Yes, it's been a tough year for many, a tough time all round. But is there cause for optimism? Absolutely.

I did say, in Images 2008: 'Beat that, 2009'. Do you know, in spite of the economic climate, I think we did.

i33 / Foreword
Peter Till / Illustrator

Manchester born Peter Till read English Literature at Cambridge University. He has been an illustrator since 1969 and has had work published in books, magazines and newspapers here and in the USA, France, Germany, Holland, South Africa and Australia. He is a member of the AGI (Alliance Graphique Internationale) an affiliation of the world's leading graphic designers and artists and a patron of the AOI.

One sunny day in the summer of 1969 I went to Notting Hill Gate with a slim portfolio of black and white drawings. I hadn't been to art school and, although I was making drawings, I was also writing and performing in an underground theatre group called The Flies. I visited the offices of Time Out and Oz magazine which were in the same road. Both publications bought a drawing from my portfolio. I mentally leapt into the air and clicked my heels. This is good I thought. These were magazines in which the text and the illustration didn't have to relate to each other much or even at all. Also you could never be sure, in the case of Oz, whether your drawing would be featured or hidden behind the copy on a psychedelic magenta and acid green page. Such was my almost random route into illustration. It contrasts starkly with the way that illustrators must now approach what I suppose we have to call the market place: with plump portfolios of incredibly accomplished artwork, calling cards, brochures, websites. Things sure have tightened up in the intervening years.

But what market forces have not done is suppress the ingenuity of illustration. It is more diverse in style and methodology than it has ever been. This should not surprise us. Every innovation makes the graphic vocabulary available that much richer. And the computer has only broadened still further the range of tools at the artist's fingertips. That illustration serves commerce does nothing to stifle the superabundant energy of the artistic outpouring that can be seen between these pages. Indeed the sometimes dry nature of the subject matter that one is illustrating means that it is to the artist that an editor looks for wit or drama or invention.

I always loved illustration and graphic art in general: how it could distil a complex idea into a witty image, the promiscuous way it borrowed from whatever idiom was most germane, the candid use of symbols and logos as props in a graphic stage set, the surrealistic yoking together of disparate elements to invite the viewer to form an interpretation of the image, the irreverent appropriation of art history and tradition. All this is ably demonstrated in these pages.

There are some surprises. Several images would not look out of place in my collection of Graphis magazine from the 1950s. No bad thing. Scraperboard is still being (tellingly) used. Flat colour, mechanically applied, is not universal!

This book is testimony to an artistic exuberance that shows no sign of flagging.

i33 / Judges

The marks awarded by the jury for originality,
artistic ability and fulfilment of the brief
determined which images were given an award or
invited to feature in the book.

i33 / Judges
Jason Ford / Malcolm Garrett / Margaret Hope

Jason Ford / Illustrator
Jason has been working as a freelance illustrator for almost 20 years helping to set up the illustration studio collective, 'Big Orange', along the way.

A diet of Tintin, Fred Quimby and comics as a child and a continuing love of classic French 'bande desinee' have contributed to Jason's approach to image making. A clear line, a simplified palette and ideas peppered with wit have kept him in constant demand.

Jason has worked for numerous clients including The Royal Mail, American Airlines, Orange, Vodafone, Science Museum, Penguin, Random House, The Guardian, The Times.

Category / Self Promotion and Design
"I found the quality of work varied enormously from amateur to highly accomplished. The winning images stood out almost immediately and the panel appeared to be unanimous in their judging criteria. Engaging concepts, competent image making coupled with energy, wit and charm. I especially enjoyed Jonas Bergstrand's 'Paper Street Collage' for its inventiveness and Olivier Kugler's 'Sustainability Drawings' for their graphic draughtsmanship."

Malcolm Garrett RDI / Creative Director, Applied Information Group
Malcolm has designed for all manner of arts, communications, and entertainment media. His work with Buzzcocks, Duran Duran, Simple Minds and Peter Gabriel in the 70s and 80s is widely regarded as having a seminal influence on contemporary graphic design. For the last two decades he has been particularly concerned with user-experience and interface design for interactive media.

Category / New Media, New Talent and Children's Books
"Whilst the AOI awards show once again that there is no shortage of talent out there, I'd hoped to see more submissions where illustrators had risen to the new media challenge and shown much more interest in web-based animation and interactivity."

Margaret Hope / Art Director, Random House Children's Books
Margaret Hope is Children's Art Director at Random House. Moving South of the border in the mid 80s, she worked in a number of different industries, including advertising and licensed properties/gift. Margaret has spent the last twenty years in children's publishing, following a strong vocational calling. She has worked on a varied range of book genres and age ranges. As a global industry, Children's Publishing, has provided Margaret with the opportunity of working with artists from all over the world, as well as nurturing home grown talent. Margaret lives and works in London, with her husband Nigel, son Rory and five cats.

Category / Children's Books, New Talent and New Media
"Standard of work submitted was very high, which made it a pleasure to judge, but also a challenging task. Well done to all the contributors, the book will look amazing and we have you to thank. Great to meet the other judges, all passionate about art and from such a variety of design industries. Funny thing is, we all had very similar tastes on what appealed to us the most! Amazing feat by AOI, organising the judging. Well organised and a pleasure to work with such a knowledgeable and dedicated team. Military precision. Thanks guys."

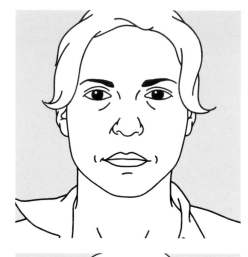

Nat Hunter / Managing Director, Airside
Nat is co-founder of digital/design/ illustration/animation agency Airside. Airside has created award-winning illustration-based work for clients such as Fiat, Nokia, Greenpeace, Vitsoe, Orange and Surf. They use illustration for its unique ability to communicate difficult subjects in a memorable and amusing way.

In 2007 Nat co-founded the not-for-profit social enterprise Three Trees Don't Make A Forest - which aims to help the design industry produce sustainable creative work. She has also judged the D&AD and Design Week awards, and has served on NESTA's fellowship panel.

Category / Design and Self Promotion
"The judging was fun and really interesting. We chose Olivier Kugler for the Gold prize as he has such a unique and dynamic way of telling a story."

Choi Liu / Art Buyer, M&C Saatchi
Choi Liu has been an Art Buyer for the last 14 years. Choi's main responsibility is sourcing creative talents for all of M&C Saatchi's clients as well as occasionally helping out international offices such as Paris, Berlin, LA, Hong Kong and Sydney.

She thrives on the daily challenges, constantly on the lookout for something new and original and dosen't limit herself to just the UK. Choi views portfolios on a daily basis which average around five portfolios per day and gets a tremendous thrill when she discovers something really special – which really is not that often.

Category / Design and Self Promotion
"I thoroughly enjoyed the experience of judging Images 33. I was particularly drawn to those illustrations which had originality."

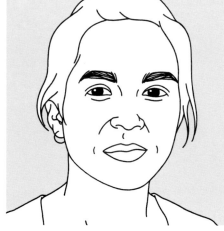

Gavin Morris / Freelance Designer
Gavin has been designing books for the past six years, initially for HarperCollins in the US and then back across the pond at Transworld. He went freelance three years ago and loves designing book covers and the process of commissioning illustration. He has worked across the publishing spectrum for most of the large publishing houses like Random House and Little, Brown to the smaller independents such as Faber, Short Books, Atlantic and Serpent's Tail. He loves discovering new illustration talent and is always on the lookout at the degree shows.

Category / Books, Editorial and Advertising
"I was very pleased to judge this years AOI selection and found it interesting to see what's going on in advertising and editorial as well as book design. A few people really stood out from the crowd across each of the three areas and made the judging a really pleasurable experience."

Maggie Murphy / Art Director, Guardian Weekend Magazine
Maggie Murphy graduated from Carlisle College, specialising in editorial design. She then went to Redwood Publishing to work on BBC Gardener's World. From there she freelanced at Sunday Times Magazine and Vogue. She joined The Guardian in 1998 and has been Art Director of Weekend magazine for the last 6 years.

Category / Editorial, Advertising and Books
"If anything, the movement in 2008 has been a return to the more detailed, evocative images and away from the stark, purely graphic style that has saturated the market for a few years, and I welcome this."

Stuart Outhwaite / Art Director, Mother
Stuart grew up in the North East in a town called Hexham with his family, John, Jessica, Ted and Lydia. After school he went to Buckinghamshire Chilterns University College to study Graphics & Advertising. He was then lucky enough to be given the opportunity to work at the advertising agency Mother where he has since worked for the last six years. He enjoys football, socialising and writing in the third person.

Category / New Talent, Children's Books and New Media
"I'm going to be up front with you all; I can't draw for toffee - not even the cheap 20p 'after swimming club' treat type. I'm in bloody advertising for God's sake, so what do I know. With such inarguable fact in mind, I judged each and every illustration by thinking 'Would I stick it on my fridge door?'. I'm sorry if you disagree with my decisions and particularly sorry to all those whose pieces featured rotten fish or anything resembling the colours of Sunderland F.C."

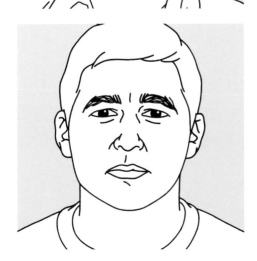

Richard Robinson / Art Director, Leo Burnett
Having dragged himself through art college in Lincoln, then advertising college in High Wycombe, Richard was lucky enough to land himself a plum job as an art director at Bartle Bogle Hegarty. He stayed for almost 10 years before being lured away in 2008 by Leo Burnett. He rarely picks up a pencil anymore. Instead, he spends his days looking at lovely pictures that other people have made, extolling their virtues to his visually-backward writing partner, Graham.

Category / Advertising, Editorial and Books
"I'm always impressed by the diversity of illustration and its ability to constantly re-invent itself, and this body of work stays true to that beautifully."

Barry Miles, born 1943, spent four years at Gloucestershire College of Art before moving to London in 1963. In 1966 he was the co-founder of Indica Books and Gallery where John Lennon first met Yoko Ono. That same year Miles was co-founder of International Times (IT), the first European underground newspaper where his first four interviews were with Paul McCartney, George Harrison, Mick Jagger and Pete Townshend. He attended Beatles recording sessions and the famous 'All You Need Is Love' world telecast. In 1968 Paul McCartney appointed him head of Zapple, the Beatles' spoken word label.

He specialises in writing about the Beat Generation and is the author of Allen Ginsberg: A Biography,1989; William Burroughs: El Hombre Invisible, 1992; Jack Kerouac: King of the Beats, 1998; Beat Hotel, 2000, etc.. His best selling Paul McCartney: Many Years From Now, 1997 was written in close collaboration with McCartney. His illustrated books include Hippie, 2003; Peace, 50 Years of the Peace Symbol, 2008, and numerous rock biographies.

To be asked to choose the image that you like the best from a selection of about 400 is a daunting task because normally one does not make that sort of value judgement when looking through a magazine or book. It was fascinating to pay close attention to pictures that are normally seen in other contexts, you see details that are normally missed. It was a very enjoyable experience, like visiting a group show at a gallery. In the event my choice was easy.

I have written a number of books about the American Beat Generation writers so I was immediately attracted to Sarah Hanson's design for a new cover for the Penguin edition of On the Road. It initially reminded me of a Rauschenberg, an artist of the same period as Kerouac; her sense of composition and tonality is similar to his and she walks the eye around the image using many of his techniques though I'm sure she arrived at these solutions from a different route. She has paid close attention to detail showing a familiarity with the subject: Carolyn Cassady's famous portrait of Neal Cassady (the hero, under the name of Dean Moriarty, of the book) and Jack Kerouac is cropped to make it balance the other elements; the Golden Gate Bridge is shown from the San Francisco side, leading out of the city, to the open road; Mel's Drive-In is another iconic symbol of fifties American car culture, as is the 1950 Hudson, a model once owned by Neal Cassady, the ultimate symbol of movement.

The book was written in 1951 about events in the late forties but not published until 1957 so the time period captured is just right. The route taken in the main journey in the book is literally mapped on the cover and the overall ochre brown hue gives the image a tinge of nostalgia, of a lost past. Though a mix-media collage, she has respected the picture plane which enables her to lead the eye to the centre of the picture, to a distant point, miles away, as if going on a journey.

This image could have been produced as an artist's print: in fact there is little to separate illustration from so-called fine art these days except perhaps that illustrators are usually responding to a commission, but then, so were many of the prints made by Matisse and Picasso.

Sarah Hanson lives and works just outside London as an illustrator. She graduated in 2006 with a BA in Graphic Design and Illustration from the University of Hertfordshire. Since then her work has attracted commissions from international clients including British Airways, Renault, BBC Worldwide, HarperCollins, Penguin, and Publicis (Belgium). She has worked on a range of advertising, design, publishing and editorial projects.

Sarah's work is a combination of traditional hand-made and digital collage. Inspired by her travels and an avid collector of random ephemera, she finds and stores old papers, maps, and photographs, which have all become strong elements in her work.

Sarah's compositional treatment of landscapes imbue her images with a strong sense of place attracting, among others, many travel related projects notably Stephen Fry's recent book 'In America'.

Sarah Hanson / On The Road
Section Books
Medium Collage
Brief Produce a cover illustration for Jack Kerouac's book "On The Road" to represent the journey of Sal and friend Dean as they travel across America.
Commissioned by Sirida Pensri
Client Penguin

Work commissioned for advertising purposes
appearing in print and digital media, also
television advertising both products and events.

i33 / Advertising / Essay
Jim Davies / Writer and Cultural Commentator

Jim Davies is a commercial writer and cultural commentator. He's helped clients like Paul Smith, Orange, Royal Mail and Waterstone's with everything from naming and one-liners to ads, books, web sites and annual reports. His articles have appeared in specialist design and advertising titles including Eye, Print, Campaign and Design Week as well as the Guardian, Daily Telegraph, Financial Times and Sunday Times Magazine. In 2008, he was awarded the creative industry's top award – a D&AD Gold – for his contribution to the National Gallery's 'Grand Tour', conceived by the Partners. He has sat on creative juries for D&AD, BAFTA and Design Week.

The days when commercial artists ruled the waves in advertising are long gone. The golden age of the illustrated poster was back in the early 20th century… AM Cassandre elegantly invited punters aboard steam liners or to sip on a Dubonnet; John Hassall's jolly fat man urged tourists to travel to bracing Skegness; John Gilroy was embarking on a remarkable 35-year run in which he produced over 100 classic posters for Guinness.

But gradually, exciting, new-fangled media superseded the allure of illustration. First photography, and then more tellingly television, saw commercial illustration relegated from star billing to occasional novelty act. Since the 1950s – barring the odd aberration – illustration has been struggling to make itself heard as advertising creatives frantically chase whatever happens to be the latest and greatest thing.

Ironically, it's technology that has helped illustration make something of a comeback of late. Simple, flat illustration has proved just the ticket to bring character to online branding and advertising. More flexible and less memory hungry than photography, this style of cartoonesque illustration has been used effectively by the Italian white goods manufacturer Zanussi. Here, Spencer Wilson has provided his characteristically big-headed characters on bright yellow backgrounds in a charming campaign that works as well online as it does in press and poster formats.

Other technology-based brands and their agencies have recognised the humanising power of illustration. For some time now, the mobile phone company Orange has been adept at using illustration to create a warm, cuddly feeling around the brand by commissioning hand-picked illustrators like Richard Levesley and Graham Carter, and building a strong bank of imagery to be drawn on where necessary. The volume of leaflets, direct mail and tactical advertising spawned by a large company like Orange is scary, and illustration provides a quick and relatively cheap option. With a strong colour and typographic template, Orange are not afraid to mix and match styles, though the illustration they favour tends towards the bold and graphic end of the spectrum.

More broadly, faux naïf illustrators like Paul Davis and Tom Gauld have been embraced by the ad industry for their ability to make big corporations appear more approachable, and to put over ideas quickly and directly. Their stick-like characters could almost have been dawn by the man in the street, which makes them easy to relate to. These figures are distinctly non-threatening, as Davis' image of a criminal in a Met Police ad demonstrates, and have a lightness of touch which provides the perfect foil for serious messages like Gauld's recent Boots campaign.

The other area where advertising illustration has and will continue to thrive is pastiche. Stella Artois' recent campaign through Lowe London featured an impeccable take on the classic 1920s and 1930s French poster genre by David Lawrence. The arresting, dusty-archive look was achieved in a refreshingly low-tech manner using stencil paper and brushes – this not only brought authenticity to the images, but gave them the required richness and depth to work at poster scale.

The icing on the cake last year was seeing illustration starring in two high-profile television commercials. In BBH's ad for Persil Small & Mighty, a child explains how the product uses less energy to make it, less packaging and less lorries to deliver it using a dinky illustrated pop up book. When was the last time you saw paper engineering celebrated on prime-time television? And mobile phone manufacturer Nokia used a host of illustrators and a stop-frame film technique to show a hand-drawn map the size of a park gradually taking shape – an imaginative and vivid demonstration of its new GPS mapping service.

How gratifying to see illustration finally finding a way of turning the tables on television, its greatest nemesis.

Artbombers is an image-making studio run by Simon Spilsbury and Richard Chant with an ambition to produce striking images that are relevant and effective but also have longevity. The partners' backgrounds cover all aspects of the visual media from advertising to editorial, and new media to TV animation. They have an international client list and their work has been awarded by D&AD, Creative Circle, Campaign Press/Poster, American Illustration, Print Magazine, 3x3 Magazine, Communication Arts, Epica, The One Show and now British Illustration.

Hair

Medium Mixed media
Brief To bring comedy back to the seaside.
Commissioned by John Messum
Client Farm
Commissioned for Paramount Comedy Channel

1 Roughs
2 Work in situ

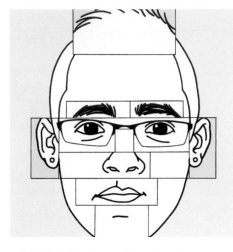

Mcfaul is big, but small: a boutique design agency with a global sneaker-sized footprint. 'We're a cherry-picked elite squad of creative talent. And the design? It is design in its broadest sense; a full service: graphic design, animation, online, film-making, art direction and more. Any material, any surface, any challenge' As long as the project is interesting, they're game.

'Our client portfolio reads like a who's who of global high-fliers. Nokia, Lucasfilm, Sony, Toshiba, Nike, Vodafone, Carhartt, Levi's, Samsung and Orange: some of the names who stand by the McFaul flag. Which we like to wave. Quite a lot.'

Medium Paint
Brief To kick off a new campaign and generate buzz, BBDO New York commissioned building-size murals at multiple locations around New York City such as the corners of 6th and Grand, Prince and Mulberry, West Broadway and Canal, etc. Giant, 3-D rubber "thongs" (they actually call them "thongs") and corresponding white outlines were then placed over these murals to, quite literally, capture the spirit of the colorful Brazilian brand.
Commissioned by Bronwen Gilbert
Client BBDO NY
Commissioned for Havaianas

i33 / Advertising / Bronze
Nishant Choksi / Winter Roaming

Nishant works for a range of clients across the advertising, book publishing and editorial fields. He has created images for many of the major UK magazines and newspapers, and most recently worked on a prominent advertising campaign for Vodafone, which appeared in stores and on billboards globally as well as being animated for television.

His work with JWT on the Berocca press advert was short listed for a D&AD award and was a winner of two creative circle awards in 2008.

Nishant participated in a successful four person show at the Coningsby Gallery in London, and is currently working on a children's book project with Macmillan

Nishant lives and works in Brighton with his wife and children.

Medium Digital
Brief Print ad created for Vodafone's Global airports campaign. The theme was Winter Roaming.
Commissioned by Mark Reddy
Client BBH
Commissioned for Vodafone

Work commissioned for adult books,
fiction and non-fiction, book jackets
and interior illustrations.

i33 / Books / Essay
Will Webb / Designer and Illustrator

Graduating from Newcastle Polytechnic with a joint degree in Design and Illustration, Will Webb has worked in and around publishing for almost twenty years, eleven of those as Art Director at Bloomsbury Publishing. He currently runs his own design company in London and occasionally illustrates books.

As the resurgence in illustrated book covers continues unabated the division of roles between 'designer' and 'illustrator' seems to be, in many cases, increasingly less distinct.

Some of the most interesting and iconic illustrated book covers of the last few years have not always been the work of so-called illustrators at all, but often it is the work of designers and art directors; people who would perhaps hesitate to describe themselves as illustrators or their work as illustration. Jonathan Gray has produced many iconic illustrated covers, as has Nathan Burton (Wildwood by Roger Deakin, Zadie Smith's On Beauty). David Pearson illustrated many of the covers for the Great Loves series that he designed for Penguin, the list goes on, David Wardle, Yeti McCaldin, Coralie Bickford Smith, Katie Tooke, myself and many others...

This of course works both ways and it is certainly not hard to find illustrators whose work includes lettering and type, sometimes to the exclusion of anything else.

One only need to look at the relatively short history of book covers (and make some sweeping generalisations) to see that this is not a recent phenomenon but the re-emergence of a tradition that has always existed. Looking at illustrated covers from the 1920s through to the 1950s, such artists as Edward McKnight Kauffer, Edward Bawden, Clifford and Rosemary Ellis were equally adept at handling type and image. There is often no separation between illustrator and designer, and indeed the discipline of graphic design (at least in the context of book covers) was much closer to what we would now define as illustration. The distinction between the two seems to coincide with the much more widespread use of photography on covers, starting in the 1960s (although there are still examples of art director/illustrators from this period, such as Alan Aldridge at Penguin). There are plenty of great illustrated covers from this period, but a trend appears to take shape. The re-emergence of the designer/illustrator, has, unsurprisingly, coincided with the renaissance of illustrated covers. There are several reasons why this has happened. Firstly publishers hate commissioning illustrators (they also hate commissioning photographers) – any creative process whose outcome cannot be wholly predicted is regarded with deep suspicion. The profit margins on 90% of books are tiny and blowing your cover budget on something as unknown as an illustrator is often a risk that editors are unwilling to take, so step-in the illustrating designer... . The dreaded cover meetings that most, if not all, publishers insist upon, demand visuals of such close proximity to the finished article that it often makes more sense to do it yourself. Secondly, looking for images from photo libraries and then choosing a font from the computer is, after a while, quite dull.

The computer has removed much of the physical aspect of work; but getting out the pencils, paints, ink, paper, wood, water, lino, knives, brushes, rollers etc puts that physical part of the creative process back, which, to many of us, is an essential part of the process.

Geoff Grandfield is an illustrator and academic, and since graduating from RCA in 1987 has worked for publishing, design and advertising clients including the Guardian, the Times, the Radio Times and Penguin Books. During the 1990's he led the BA Illustration at Middlesex University and is currently course director of BA illustration and animation at Kingston University.

Though Geoff has previously won Images gold for books three times, Images silver for editorial, the V&A illustration award and two D&AD yellow pencils for illustration series, he is still excited to have won gold this year.

Medium Chalk pastel and Photoshop
Brief Create a series of internal illustrations for the second Folio Society volume of Raymond Chandler's short stories.
Commissioned by Joe Whitlock-Blundell
Client The Folio Society
Commissioned for Raymond Chandler's short stories

Despotica is the illustration alter-ego of Mike Topping. Mike worked with words until he'd had enough and decided to work with pictures instead. He has studied Digital Image-Making, Illustration and Printmaking at London College of Communication, and made pictures for clients including Penguin Books, Portobello Books and Old Boy Music. His work is often macabre or humorous - sometimes both, and reflects his love of collections, curiosities, ephemera, museums, charity shops and afternoon films. He lives in London and dreams of a studio by the sea.

Medium Digital
Brief Illustrations for the front covers of eight Sherlock Holmes titles in Penguin's Red Classics range, emphasising the adventurous, sensational aspects of the stories.
Commissioned by Coralie Bickford-Smith
Client Penguin Books

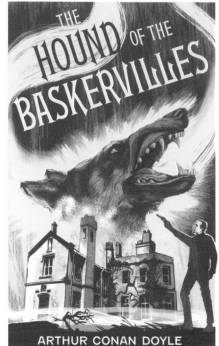

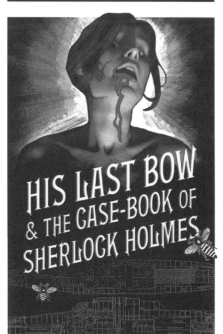

i33 / Books / Bronze
Swava Harasymowicz / Birdsong

Swava grew up in Krakow Poland, where she
studied philology. She moved to London in
1998. After stints as a translator, shop
assistant and the World Service radio
broadcast technician, she graduated from
the Royal College of Art in 2006.

Swava's work has been commissioned by
clients including BBC.co.uk, The Folio
Society, Guardian Weekend Magazine, Modern
Poetry in Translation, Penguin Books,
Randomhouse and Uniqlo. She has designed
limited edition posters exhibited in
China, Iran and Warsaw Poster biennals
throughout 2007 and 2008. She is a winner
of both categories in this year's VUA
Illustration Awards.

Her current projects include a new
series of one off screen prints and a
graphic novel.

Medium Mixed media
Brief One of nine illustrations for Birdsong by
Sebastian Faulks.
Commissioned by Eleanor Crow
Client The Folio Society

i33 / Children's Books

Work commissioned for children's books,
jackets and interior illustrations.

i33 / Children's Books / Essay

Margaret Hope / Art Director, Random House Children's Books

Margaret Hope is Children's Art Director at Random House. Moving South of the border in the mid 80s, she worked in a number of different industries, including advertising and licensed properties/gift. Margaret has spent the last twenty years in children's publishing, following a strong vocational calling. She has worked on a variety of book genres and age ranges. As a global industry, children's publishing, has provided Margaret with the opportunity of working with artists from all over the world, as well as nurturing home grown talent. Margaret lives and works in London, with her husband Nigel, son Rory and five cats.

Writing a piece about children's publishing during this uncertain economic time is challenging. By the time the 2009 AOI book of Illustration is printed in all it's glorious colour the market might have picked up, or deteriorated further. The Bologna Book Fair in April usually gives us a clear indication of how the Global market is fairing. Publishers are feeling the pinch with rising production costs, squeezed margins, increased discounts and ever shrinking market.

To counter this, the amount of new titles are being reduced and origination costs being pushed down. Printing colour Far East has always allowed us to venture into many different finishes, formats and creating novelty at affordable prices. However, that is changing with rising manufacturing costs. Where does this leave the humble illustrator and what are the consequences for creatives? Fewer original titles and publishing houses? Would it be impossible for new talent to break into children's publishing?

Publishing is an age-old industry and we've weathered recessions before. Reading, sharing and enjoying books, has always remained part of a child's development and education. Publishers offer a wide and varied range of books for young and old. Picture books and young fiction are often lavishly illustrated and as I'm sure you heard quoted before, "Even after children learn to read, illustrations continue to aid to their comprehension. Among the many components of a child's visual world, book illustrations are a beautiful medium through which to learn about their world." - Anderson. Fiction, education and picture books are core for the UK, and mass-market picture paperbacks have been enjoying a buoyant uplift. With the shrinking global market in hardback colour, UK led paperbacks are holding their own. This less expensive format allows new talent to evolve and gives quirky, contemporary art a home.

However, the classics remain the backbone to most publishing houses and hardback originals the global format. Fiction remains as strong as ever and the range of covers, formats and illustrative mediums used wide and varied. As fiction encompasses many age ranges, the scope and opportunities for illustrators are plentiful. Trends in successful sales might spawn a shop full of identical covers, however fiction also provides an outlet for truly contemporary look and content. Content is veering away from the purely conceptual approach, towards the narrative, as the audience doesn't always get the message conveyed.

Another casualty of the tightened purse strings are the whacky, wonderful finishes and gimmicks. The quality of the content, illustrative look and feel of the book is crucial. So, will there be fewer publishers and less work? The unprecedented decline in the market and rising costs will have an impact, but illustration below a certain age range is an important and integral part of a children's book. Children's publishing will always have an outlet for illustrators and their work. We're all having to work that wee bit harder, but often these harsh conditions spark wonderful new creative material.

Quoting Walt Disney, "There is more treasure in books than in all the pirate's loot on Treasure Island." That makes me, and all those who work in children's books, rich beyond our wildest dreams. Who said anything about a gloomy recession?

Poly was born in Buenos Aires, Argentina, and has been drawing ever since. He graduated from Buenos Aires' Art School, where he established a strong interest in using different techniques for his work, which has always been based on experimentation and diversity. As a result his work is constantly changing and developing, searching for new ways to tell a story.

Poly has worked across advertising, animation and comics, and over the last couple of years, has established an exciting career publishing more than 60 children's books in Argentina, Mexico, Spain, Australia, Denmark, Taiwan and Belgium.

His books have been translated into many different languages, including German, Korean, Serbian, Greek and Italian.

Recent books published in the UK include 'The Tickle Tree' and 'The Monster Diaries' (Meadowside Children's Books, 2008, 2005) and 'The Sorceror's Apprentice' (2006).

Medium Paint, collage and digital
Brief Create original complimentary illustrations for a 24-page picture book for the 3-5 age group.
Commissioned by Sarah Wilson
Client Meadowside Children's Books

The Tickle Tree

Written by **Chae Strathie**

Illustrated by
Poly Bernatene

Jonny Duddle is an illustrator living in Buxton. After studying Design at Staffordshire University, he got a proper job as a pirate. "I jumped ship in Dublin because the ship's chef didn't like my vegetarian ways, and worked as a struggling painter, a children's entertainer and a gallery warden.' Jonny then trained as a teacher, got a job in Kang, Botswana, decided it was too hot, and moved back to Manchester. He left teaching to work as a concept artist in computer games for eight years, before becoming a freelance illustrator. Nowadays Jonny illustrates children's books and designs characters for games and feature films.

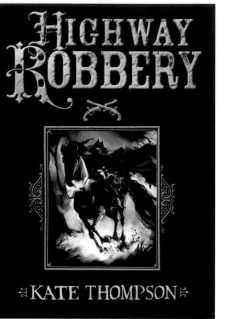

Medium Digital media
Brief To portray the infamous highwayman Dick Turpin upon his legendary steed, Black Bess, conveying speed and drama for the cover, and full page images accompanying the text for the book interior.
Commissioned by James Fraser
Client Random House Children's Books
Commissioned for Highway Robbery by Kate Thompson

i33 / Children's Books / Bronze

David Lucas / Something To Do

David Lucas was born in Middlesborough and grew up in Hackney, East London.

His first book as author and illustrator, 'Halibut Jackson' (Anderson Press), was chosen as Amazon.com's 'Favourite Children's Book of 2004' and Publishers Weekly's 'Best Children's Book of 2004'.

His most recent books are 'The Lying Carpet' (Anderson Press), a richly illustrated fable for old children; and picture books 'Something to Do' (Gullane Children's Books) and 'Peanut' (Walker Books). In 2008 he was a winner of Booktrust's Best New Illustrator Award.

He lives beside Victoria Park in London, close to where he grew up, and works in a studio nearby.

Something To Do

by David Lucas

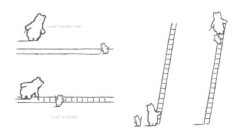

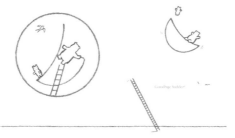

Look! A shooting star.

Medium Digital
Brief Create an original text and complimentary illustration for a 32-page picture book for the 3-5 age group.
Commissioned by Paula Burgess
Client Gullane Children's Books

i33 / Design

Work commissioned for use in packaging;
calendars; merchandising; annual reports;
stationery; brochures; catalogues and
greeting cards.

i33 / Design / Essay
Mike Dempsey / Founder, Studio Dempsey

Mike Dempsey has been around the block a bit. A graphic designer for over 40 years, he worked in publishing for ten of those and founded the design consultancy CDT in 1979. He has created everything from stamps to film title sequences and editorial design to visual identities. He is also a writer, photographer, broadcaster, painter, blogger and studied acting at the Method Studio London. In between all that he's had six children, 8 houses, 2 divorces, 5 cats and 2 dogs. Has won ten D&AD Silvers and a Gold. Elected a member of Alliance Graphic International, was President of D&AD and past Master of The Faculty of Royal Designers for Industry. He left CDT at the end of 2007 to form Studio Dempsey – an intimate space to dream and create. He lives and works in London and Dorset.

Of Mice and Pens I've been commissioning illustration for over four decades, including a stint as an illustrator myself. So I feel in a good place to comment on this wonderful creative endeavour.

One of my early jobs in the 60s was working as an in-house designer for an artist agent - an unusual situation. But their publishing clients were constantly asking if they had someone who could add the typography to the various book jackets that the illustrations had been commission for. I found myself working with illustrations from Renato Fratini, Charles Raymond, Christopher Foss, Tom Adams and many others all at the top of their game way back then. I quickly realised that the relationship between a designer and an illustrator's work is a delicate one. So many illustration projects are routinely ruined by unsympathetic layouts and typography.

I've heard stories of advertising agencies tampering with commissioned work in Photoshop to such an extent that the illustrator has disowned their work in utter despair and do little about complaining for fear that they will not be commissioned from the agency again.

I enjoy collaborating with conceptually minded illustrators and those with a distinct personality in their work. What I want in the mix is an extension of the idea in order to make it better. Grazing through this years work I was struck by the fact that they have mostly been extracted from their commissioned landscapes, be it cover, poster, book or ad. To not see work in context is an incomplete picture. I realise that space is an issue. But I suspect that some of the original scenarios might well have diminished the Illustrations effectiveness.

Brush, pencil, sponge, pen, scalpel, engraving tool and mouse all reflect the rich diversity of illustration styles included this year. The fluidity and beauty of Olivier Kugler's reportage approach in his Gold winning sustainability project demonstrates the power that simple drawing still has. Simon Pemberton's Silver, for his backdrops to the Taylors coffee packaging has the immediacy of the moving brush. While Ian Whadcock's, tabletop rowing boat and Chris Vine's, 'Maypole on the Mersey' are examples of the kind of

wit that I enjoy. That stalwart of the illustrated diagram, Peter Grundy seems to get better with the passing years and underlines that pure graphic design has its place in the world of illustration. Jessie Ford's Mothercare packaging is one of the few examples where the relationship between designer and Illustrator is perfectly balanced and included in the annual.

The unsettled economic outlook will no doubt affect illustrators, with projects being cancelled or fees being reduced. But it has happened many times before and is part of the professional life cycle of the illustrator. It's important not to lose heart. What the illustrators give to society is at times sublime and capable of lifting the spirits on a cold grey day, for which I am eternally grateful.

Olivier was born in Stuttgart, Germany, grew up in a small village in the Black Forest, and was influenced by French/Belgian bande desinées and Otto Dix. After military service in the Navy he studied graphic design in Pforzheim and worked as a designer in Karlsruhe for a few years. He got terribly bored with it and received a scholarship from the German Academic Exchange Service to do a masters in illustration at the School of Visual Arts in New York. Since then he's worked as an illustrator in London for clients all over the world.

Olivier likes to work on reportage illustrations, loving to draw people he meets and places he visits. He prefers to draw on location or from his own reference photos.

Medium Mixed media
Brief Create 20 drawings documenting the sustainability philosophy of Fletcher Priest Architects.
Commissioned by Martin Edwards
Client Fletcher Priest Architects
Commissioned for Book report

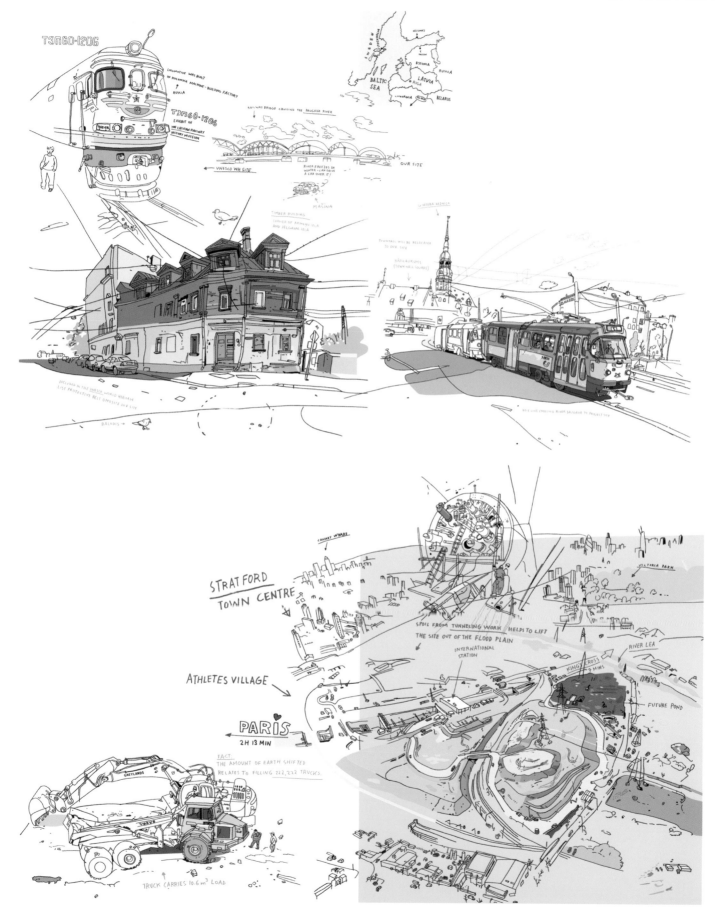

Simon was born near Liverpool and moved to London to study his MA Illustration at Central St Martins. He now lives and works in London's East End with a studio overlooking London Fields. His illustration work has been commissioned by a wide range of major design, publishing and advertising agencies worldwide. Projects are as diverse as brand development, packaging, book covers, editorial and corporate literature.

Clients include Adobe U.K, Fuji, Taylors of Harrogate, British Airways, Royal Opera House, Leith Harbour Development, CDT, Lowe, New York Times, L.A Times, Guardian, Observer, Independent, Blueprint, Financial Times, New Scientist, Tatler, Harper Collins, Penguin, Hodder, Random House Publishing, Readers Digest, BBC Worldwide….

Simon is a previous winner of two Silver awards for Books and Editorial and two Bronze awards for Design and Advertising.

Medium Mixed media
Brief Hot Lava: To capture the spirit of Hot Lava Java speciality blend coffee - a rich, dark, powerful blend with an intense caffeine kick. Fairtrade Organic: To show the rich fertile landscape of Nicaragua where this blend of smooth organically grown coffee originates. Cafe Brasilia: To create a vibrant image showing elements of a Brazilian street party to reflect the "liveliness of this rich seductive coffee". Cafe Imperial: To capture the traditional feel of Betty's Tea Rooms where this blend of coffee has been served for over 40 years.
Commissioned by Kerry Plummer
Client Pearl Fisher
Commissioned for Taylors of Harrogate

i33 / Design / Bronze
Jessie Ford / Don't Forget Range

Brighton based illustrator Jessie Ford has been busily producing her colourful compositions and quirky humour for a wide range of clients since graduating from Bath in 2002.

She first learnt the ropes whilst working as an agent at the Central Illustration Agency, scooting round London's top firms by day and drawing into the night. However Jessie's illustrations soon became very much in demand and she upped roots to breezy Brighton where she can still be found collecting beautiful scraps of paper that catch her eye and shooing off pesky seagulls.

Jessie has worked for clients in all sectors of the design industry, most recently Transport For London, Bloomsbury Books, Marie Claire and the Financial Times.

Medium Paper, paint and Mac
Brief To create a simple elephant character juggling different items.
Commissioned by Alan Dye
Client NB Studio
Commissioned for Mothercare/ELC

i33 / **Editorial**
Work commissioned for editorial purposes
in newspapers and magazines.

i33 / Editorial / Essay

Maggie Murphy / Art Director, Guardian Weekend Magazine

Maggie Murphy graduated from Carlisle College, specialising in Editorial Design. She then went to Redwood Publishing to work on BBC Gardener's World. From there she freelanced at Sunday Times Magazine and Vogue. She joined The Guardian in 1998 and has been Art Director of Weekend magazine for the last 6 years.

Sometimes it's a question of practicality when you commission an illustration rather than use a photograph. Illustrations can bring alive abstract images – if they're a good match with the writer, a good illustrator will create the mood before the reader has reached the first sentence. If you get it right an illustrator and a columnist can make a perfect marriage.

Sometimes as an art director you are aiming for something more ambitious – an illustration so striking that it will stand up the piece on its own and draw the reader in. On Guardian Weekend we occasionally use an illustration for the cover. We had an issue devoted to writers describing their most mortifying experience; on the cover we had a simple, graphic illustration by Paul Oakley of a woman blushing. It was arresting and did the job.

Another was a travel issue. Noma Bar has made a name for his wonderfully ingenious illustrations in which faces are made up of components of the story: eyes and nose made up of a pair of scissors, say. For our cover, a suitcase and its tags told a traveller's story.

I love illustrations. I love the imagination that goes into them and the way they convey an idea so economically. Among the entries in this competition, there were several illustrators I recognised immediately – their styles are unique. There was a very wide range. Some of the entries were markedly modern – flat colours, no fuss, very direct; others were more old school, in some instances deliberately echoing a familiar genre from the past.

The winner in the editorial category by Andy Smith, is retro in style, celebrating French cinema of the year of les évènements, 1968. It is reminiscent of the political posters of the period and a graceful combination of shapes and text in the cockerel's plumage.

The silver goes to another brilliant combination of letters and images – in this case much more angry and punky in mood, as befits the subject matter, the writer's disgust at a rude and unruly audience at a festival. The lines are bold and the colouring – red, black and white – a characteristic of the artist, Daniel Pudles.

Rumour, by Andrew Pavitt, is a pleasing, elusive image, quite different from the other two, incorporating two hands and two flags, setting off several trains of thought.

If anything, the movement in 2008 has been a return to the more detailed, evocative images and away from the stark, purely graphic style that has saturated the market for a few years, and I welcome this.

The illustrations I have been particularly pleased with at Guardian Weekend over the past year were a selection we had for the fiction issue, when several leading writers were asked to write a short story. Within reading the first few paragraphs, I knew which illustrator's style would match the tale. Unless an illustrator asks for my direction, I like to give as open a brief as possible; I think being too restrictive can hinder artist creativity. It's exciting, although a risk, to give them free rein. It paid off. The illustrations brought a fresh dynamism to what was essentially a summer read. One was by Kelly Dyson, whose fairy-tale style with a sinister edge I thought was ideal for Alice Sebold's story about a lone child survivor in a post-apocalyptic world. It's a tribute to Kelly that the author thought he had captured the essence of the story perfectly.

Since you can now see the work of hundreds of artists online, I quite often find myself choosing someone of whom I have never heard. And sometimes they go on and you suddenly are seeing them everywhere - a testament to what a good job they did for us.

Andy Smith studied illustration at Brighton University before completing an MA in illustration at The Royal College of Art, London. Since graduation he has worked for many worldwide clients designing campaigns for Nike, Orange, McDonalds and Mercedes and many others. His work combines illustration and typography to create images that have humour, energy and optimism, and despite often being created digitally his graphics have the tactile feel of the hand made and hand printed. His time is split between commercial work and self initiated and collaborative projects such as silkscreen printed books and posters, which are available from his website and have been exhibited in the UK, France, USA and Australia. Andy has won D&AD, AOI and Creative Circle awards for his work on advertising campaigns, book jackets and his animation. He lives and works in Hastings, East Sussex.

Medium Digital
Brief Produce an illustration that allows for various French film directors names to be incorporated into a symbol that refers back to the protest posters of may 68.
Commissioned by Chris Brawn
Client The BFI
Commissioned for Sight and Sound magazine

1 Rough
2 Work in situ

MICHEL CIMENT
NICOLAS KLOTZ
CATHERINE BREILLAT
JEAN-MICHEL FRODON
EUGENE GREEN
AGNES VARDA

LE CINEMA FRANÇAIS

THE LEGACY OF 68

Daniel was born in Paris and grew up in Brazil, the USA, and France where he studied at the Ecole Supérieure d'Arts Graphiques in Paris.

He felt at home when he moved to London in 1993, where his career as an editorial illustrator took off. He is particularly grateful to some wonderful people at The Guardian, The Economist and The New Statesman who allowed him to flourish and progress in this fulfilling profession.

'Un grand merci for this award to the Images 33 editorial jury!'

Medium Mixed media
Brief Nikita Lalwani witnessing a crowd becoming mob at a dutch comedian's performance at the Latitude festival.
Commissioned by David Gibbons
Client New Statesman
Commissioned for New Statesman's Diary section

i33 / Editorial / Bronze

Andrew Pavitt / Rumour

Having completed a degree in Fine Art
at Chelsea School of Art, London based
illustrator Andrew Pavitt worked in a
variety of different fields before plumping
for a career in illustration.

An early break-through came when a
meeting with Michael Mayhew at the National
Theatre led to a commission to produce
a poster for a production of A Midsummer
Nights Dream. The bold approach to design he
found here proved to be a lasting influence.

Andrew has spent the last five years at
the Big Orange studios in Shoreditch and has
been lucky enough to work along side some of
the most gifted names in the industry.

Whilst being a great admirer of more
traditional drawn illustration, he recognised
that for him his strengths lay in a more
paired down graphic approach, establishing a
wide client list along the way.

Medium Digital
Brief To reflect on the concept of the word
'rumour' and its potential political meanings.
Commissioned by Paul Davis
Client The Drawbridge

Work commissioned for video; film and
television; animation; character development
and interactive design.

i33 / New Media / Essay
Malcolm Garrett RDI / Creative Director, Applied Information Group

Malcolm has designed for all manner of arts, communications, and entertainment media. His work with Buzzcocks, Duran Duran, Simple Minds and Peter Gabriel in the 70s and 80s is widely regarded as having a seminal influence on contemporary graphic design. For the last two decades he has been particularly concerned with user-experience and interface design for interactive media.

Macintosh icon by Susan Kare.

Cosmic Osmo created by Cyan Inc., Osmo in one of the many rooms in which to explore and interact.

Apple iPhone The phone senses its position allowing direct physical interaction with the screen. Application shown: aMaze! by Simiotica

Orange Unlimited website The screen scrolls down and down and down to reveal an endless number of animated games delivering information about Orange. Website by Poke.

I've been working in interactive media for almost twenty years, yet the emerging technologies of recent years are ensuring that working and creating with New Media is still as exciting as it ever was.

In the very early days onscreen illustration was limited to bitmapped black and white images, and simple animated loops. Nevertheless, the work of Susan Kare in creating the basic Macintosh icons, using a simple grid of 32 pixels square, set the highest standard for the use of illustration in digital media. This was important not just in developing the interface itself, but it helped establish a visual environment that today offers creative opportunities unparalleled in any other media, whether printed or filmed. In fact all other media have become increasingly dependent upon this digital framework.

A charming example of how new technology precipitates new creativity was the ground-breaking 'Cosmic Osmo' (1992). Distributed on floppy disc, its interactive world was explored by clicking active elements in a sequence of inter-related images. Things have come a long way since then, and computers are now no longer constrained by such poor resolution and basic interactivity. At the very apex of interface development is iPhone, where, in one small step, Apple have again rewritten the rules. Almost by stealth they have introduced a computer you can carry with you, and where the user is moved that much closer to the screen and thus to the content. The screen may be even smaller than that of the very first Macintosh, but its power to deliver information and interactivity to your fingertips is remarkable.

With iPhone there is a real opportunity to create illustration that you can hold, touch and physically play with. All the conventional tenets of illustration still apply but, with the multi-touch screen, navigation through visual material is made dramatically easier, and more fun. Arguably the most important feature is the 'accelerometer' embedded in the hardware. Simply put this detects which way up the phone is, and thus allows anything on the screen to appear to react to gravity, as well as sound and motion. The ability to work creatively in a space that not only displays a third dimension, but actively embraces it, offers nothing short of a fundamental leap into the future.

When invited to judge the New Media category I was expecting to see how illustrators had risen to these challenges, but sadly the submissions in this category hadn't embraced interactivity as I understand it. I was hoping for more than digitally produced animation (which is not exactly new) or simple redrawing of website menus. I was looking for vibrant illustration that operates in several dimensions, engaging the viewer in active participation, with user-interactivity at its heart.

By way of example, the type of work that could expect awards include the Orange Unlimited website, which presents an endlessly scrolling screen of games and animations, in a delightful integration of technology, illustration and information. And there are already any number of iPhone applications that would qualify.

I know there is lots more great stuff out there. The challenge is how to ensure that it is submitted next year, so that this category really does represent new media. I would love to see genuinely dynamic work rewarded, yet for the moment I am left with a sense that the best has yet to be seen.

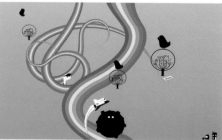

Influenced by reading too many 2000AD
comics, drawing large scale dogfights on A3
paper and loving Battle of the Planets as
much as Henry's cat, Mark has worked across
the still and moving image fields. He has
worked in the illustration/animation/
multimedia industry for clients such as
MTV, Vh1, BBC, Mother Advertising, Fallon,
Abbey Road Studios, The Guardian, The Times
and John Brown Publishing, always looking
to create work that has some kind of
atmosphere, and seeking the visual gag in a
conceptual idea or text

Mark's influences come from comic artists
such as Jack Kirby and David Mazzucchelli.
Drawing has always been the core process of
his image making, and coming from the Black
Country has also been an influence on his
work with its 'just get on with attitude'.
Mark is an active founding member of
illustration collective Black Convoy.

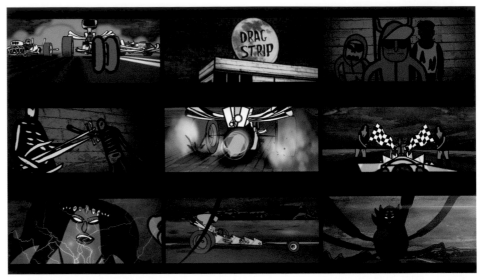

Medium Drawn/Digital
Brief DoesItOffendYou, Yeah? JimmyBoy, M.Organ and
DanitOffendyou, three undead dragracers chance upon the
Dragstrip nightclub and get down to zombierave and race
for the affections of big mama - a cliffhanger with 'too
many legs under the table'
Commissioned by Jane Skinner
Client Virgin Records
Commissioned for DoesItOffendYou, Yeah?

Ginny is half of a directing partnership with Garth Jones, who she met at Newport University in Wales. It was here, in 2005, where she graduated with a BA in Animation and picked up the IFSW 'Best Design' award for her short film 'Milk'. After which, she worked mainly as a freelance animator in London, before teaming up with Garth to join Tandem films as directing duo 'Garth + Ginny'. Their joint work to date includes the e-sting 'Headphone Jack', which played on e4, and 'Pixel Film: (?}' which toured with the Pictoplasma Character Design festival 2008/2009.

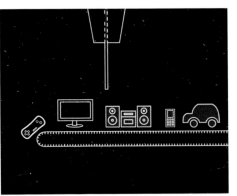

Medium Flash Animation
Brief Stills from an animated film explaining 23red's view of the way advertising — and the world — are changing. The complete animation can be seen at: 23red.com/thinking.
Commissioned by Philippa Dunning
Client 23red

i33 / New Media / Bronze
Cristina Guitian / Graphic Cowboy

Wonderfully absurd reflections of the world define the work of Cristina Guitian. With a keen interest in the power of scale, she works at the extremes - from small drawings to massive mural-installations.

Her imperfect line sketches characters that celebrate individuality and evolution. Most of the time she can be found exploring her symbolic language via personal projects which have been exhibited in Barcelona, New York, Tokyo and Amsterdam. Inevitably this research informs her commercial work, and Cristina's clients range from small local projects to giant global brands like Nike, Virgin and Diesel.

Originally from colourful Spain, Cristina is based in London and draws inspiration from its energy, scale and diversity.

Medium Ink pen
Brief 'Graphic Cowboy' is one of a series of illustrations created for Virgin Media's portfolio to help explain concepts related to creativity in the digital environment. 'Graphic Cowboy' is part of the recruitment section, reflecting the everyday work of an interactive designer/developer. The brief was to demonstrate, in one drawing, all the different aspects of the field: the creativity involved, the technological know-how required, everyday duties, and as well a deeper more general insight into the subject.
Commissioned by Virgin Media

i33 / Self Promotion

Unpublished experimental work and personal
promotional work, including speculative
publishing projects and work rejected or
not used by a client.

i33 / Self Promotion / Essay

Linda Boyle / Art Director, You Magazine

Linda Boyle has been Art Director at You Magazine for 10 years, evolving the hugely successful magazine through several re-designs. Previously she has freelanced for most monthlies including Marie Claire and Vogue. Prior to freelancing, Linda was Art Director at Redwood Publishing focusing on new launches. She is also a part time film-maker whose films have been acclaimed internationally.

With the increased use of the internet, self-promotion has changed dramatically. I still receive promotional material by post, but generally it is now by e-mail including a web-link, which is my preferred medium.

If I like the illustrator's work, I pass their details to my team to commission. Where possible I always try to respond to all e-mails, but sometimes, due to work demands, it just isn't possible.

Over the years I have been sent many kinds of self-promotion, but have found one of the most effective to be the desk-top calendar.

In particular I have used the illustrators agent CIA's calendar for the last two years. It is basic, does not come in a plastic box – so eco friendly – just simply a peel-off weekly illustration. I often give the pages to my designers to commission, and/or keep a favourite one for a later date. I find this an effective promotion without feeling bombarded by it, which can be off-putting.

Some creatives do not realise that when they send their samples to an Art Director, that said Art Directors receive many such things. It can be irritating, and therefore discouraging, if one is cold-called regarding a promotional piece that they expect you to remember off the top of your head. Also, that when calling, some people do not realise that the Art Director could be in the middle of something urgent and/or important and therefore can not chat. This can easily put one off commissioning the caller, even if you liked their work. Calling too many times, being over familiar and getting names wrong can have the same effect.

Having said all that, I have had some lovely self-promotion through the post. As all illustration is subjective, this obviously relates solely to my feelings regarding it. Here are some examples which I have liked and have in most cases led to commissions:

An illustrator we regularly use, Cyrus Deboo, sent my team a calendar in the form of an illustrated monthly postcard. We all looked forward to the next card with anticipation. This expensive promotion proved effective, as we subsequently gave Cyrus several commissions.

I've received a charming coaster size booklet from Gemma Robinson featuring biscuits waiting to be dunked into tea, and I am still using the coaster for my tea. I expect to give Gemma a suitable commission as a result. Illustration storage can be a problem, so practical items like this can be effective.

A sweet hand-drawn locket on a piece of twine arrived from Hannah Rollings featuring two portraits inside. I haven't used Hannah before, but am encouraged to give her a suitable commission soon.

So, in conclusion, I advise being practical, don't pester or waste busy people's time, do your homework, i.e. look at the type of illustration used within the publications being approached, and get the commissioner's names correct.

Most of all, be creative and be yourself.

Jonas was born and lives in Stockholm, Sweden. Unlike Indiana Jones he's a reluctant traveller, but with the internet he can still take part in the action. He joined the Central Illustration Agency from afar in 2000, and as distances are no longer so important, and since Sweden is a big importer of British culture he's up to speed and can relate to clients needs. 'England is also constantly invaded by tourists so lucky for me you're used to weird sounding accents.'

Jonas has worked with a wide range of assignments in most medias. He usually doesn't enter into competitions, but Images is the exception. He really enjoys the book and often returns to past editions for inspiration, and the idea that other illustrators might do the same and stumble across his images is very entertaining for him.

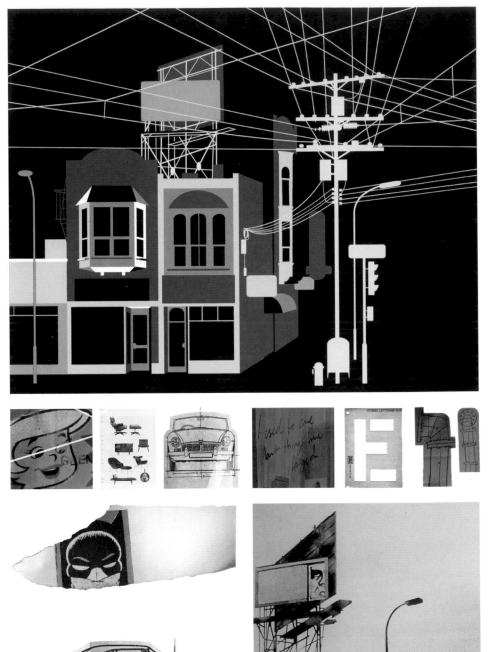

Medium Digital and Photoshop
Brief Collage made from scanned drawings, textures and photos. All put together in Photoshop.

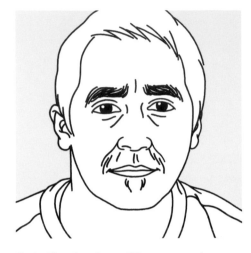

Chris Thornley is an illustrator and designer. He also goes by the name Raid71 'Which was my secret identity until now!'

He spent many of his younger days in the local woods, building camps and dams in streams, always arriving home covered head to toe in mud. 'The moors and woodlands of where I grew up heavily inspire my work.'

Chris studied at Blackburn Art College and then Gwent University; he currently works at Source Creative on a range of projects from both local and international clients.

Medium Digital
Brief Passion through storytelling.

i33 / Self Promotion / Bronze

Greg McLeod / Codswallop

Greg McLeod is one half of the award winning 'Brothers McLeod'. From surreal animated creatures to iconic characters, his work has been seen around the globe, in exhibitions from Wolverhampton to Arizona. His client list includes Aardman, Guinness, BBC, MTV, Channel 4, Nickelodeon and The Tate.

As the illustration and animation half of The Brothers McLeod he has been recognised for his design and animated works at the London Film Festival, Pictoplasma Berlin and Annecy, and has also illustrated a number of books.

There is a strong strand of the subconscious in McLeod's work, layered with a deliberate attempt to organise his illustrations and images into a coherent working whole.

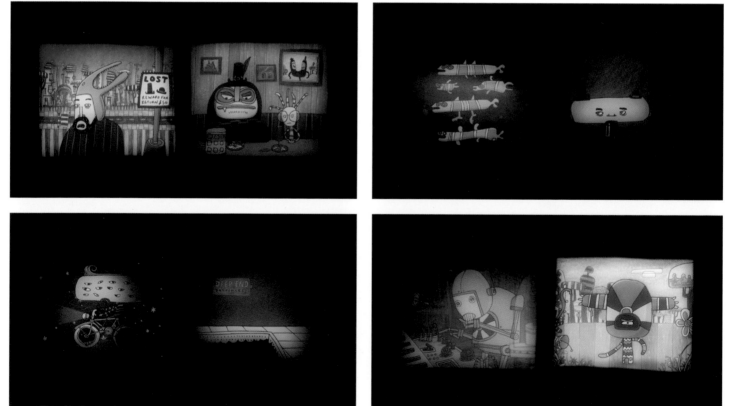

Medium Ink and coloured pencil
Brief To create a film that would stand alongside our commercial work and showcase our work on the festival circuit. Nominated for a BAFTA in 2009.

i33 / Selected Works

Each entry is marked by the jury according
to how well the work fulfils the brief,
originality, and technical ability. Only
the highest scoring images are invited to
feature in the annual.

Ulla Puggaard /
Make Love Not War
Section Editorial
Medium Paint
Brief S magazine is a bi-annually art-
erotic-fashion magazine. Theme: Desire.
Client S magazine

Jonny Hannah /
Mr. Gerry Mulligan / **Mingus Says**
Section Self Promotion
Medium Screenprint
Brief Create a series of prints
for an exhibition coinciding with a
jazz festival.

Hats Off To Hardy
Section Editorial
Medium Digital collage
Brief Illustrate a general appreciation
of the writer Thomas Hardy.
Commissioned by Alex MacFadyen
Client The Sunday Telegraph

Daniela Jaglenka Terrazzini /
Bottle Green
Section Design
Medium Ink and digital
Brief To design stylised fruits and
flowers to go on the new labels for the
Bottle Green drinks.
Commissioned by
Clara Piggot and Hayley Bishop
Client Ziggurat
Commissioned for Bottle Green

Gemma Watson /
War Of The Worlds
Section Self Promotion
Medium Digital
Brief Illustrate a chapter from War of
the Worlds.

John Bradley /
Little Red Riding Hood
Section Children's Books
Medium Ink and digital
Brief Illustrate 'Little Red Riding Hood'.
Commissioned by Lorna Heaslip
Client Richmond Publishing

Digger
Section Editorial
Medium Ink and digital
Brief Illustrate with humour solving the
problems of digging an underwater trench.
Commissioned by Dave Walters
Client Findlay Publications
Commissioned for Eureka Magazine

Scott Balmer /
A Lumberjack's Dream
Section Self Promotion
Medium Cut paper and fine liners
Brief Design a piece referencing nature
and human interaction.

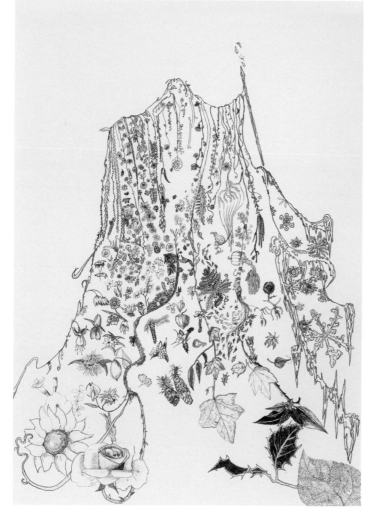

<

Christey Johansson /
Chasing Coin – The 9am Monkey Shuffle
Section Editorial
Medium Vector
Brief '9am Monkey Shuffle' is a part
of the satirical series 'Chasing
Coin', which depicts the ludicrous and
strange activities completed all in the
name of economics. This piece 'Monkey
Shuffle' depicts the morbidly comical
& overwhelming movement of the masses
during peak in Central London. The brief
included a limited size (A3) and colour
palette - Pantone 153c and 476c.
Commissioned by Greg Beer
Client Edtn Magazine
Commissioned for Group Exhibition at
Bodhi Gallery, Brink Lane

Alexandre Barre /
The Umbrella Tree: Drapée /
The Umbrella Tree in the Village
Section Self Promotion
Medium Pencil
Brief From the children's book "The
Umbrella Tree": To illustrate a fantasy
Mother Nature.

Tim Stevens
Through Day And Night
Section Self Promotion
Medium Pen and watercolour
Brief To illustrate a scene from the classic Hans Andersen fairy tale The Snow Queen. '... and the reindeer bounded through the forest, over briers and bushes, over swamps and plains, meadows and moors, through day and night'.

The Robber Woman
Section Self Promotion
Medium Pen and ink
Brief To illustrate a scene from the classic Hans Andersen fairy tale The Snow Queen. "Towards noon she will drink a little from the great bottle and after that she will sleep. Then I will do something for you".

Barbara Vagnozzi
Zelda Zebra
Section Self Promotion
Medium Acrylic on paper
Brief A series of board books with Zelda
having fantastic adventures.

Mark Barnes /
Have A Heart!
Section Self Promotion
Medium Digital
Brief Promotional Christmas card sent to
past and prospective clients.

Cate James /
So Be The Verse /
Why Did I Dream About You Last Night? /
Maiden Name
Section Self Promotion
Medium Collage and digital collage
Brief Illustration of Philip Larkin poetry.

Stephen Waterhouse
50 Favourite Bible Stories
Section Children's Books
Medium Digital
Brief To illustrate 50 stories from the
old and the new testaments that were
selected by Sir Cliff Richard and retold
by Brian Sibley.
Commissioned by Lois Rock
Client Lion Children's Books
Commissioned for A children's Bible

VINTAGE **WILDE**

THE
PICTURE
OF
DORIAN
GRAY

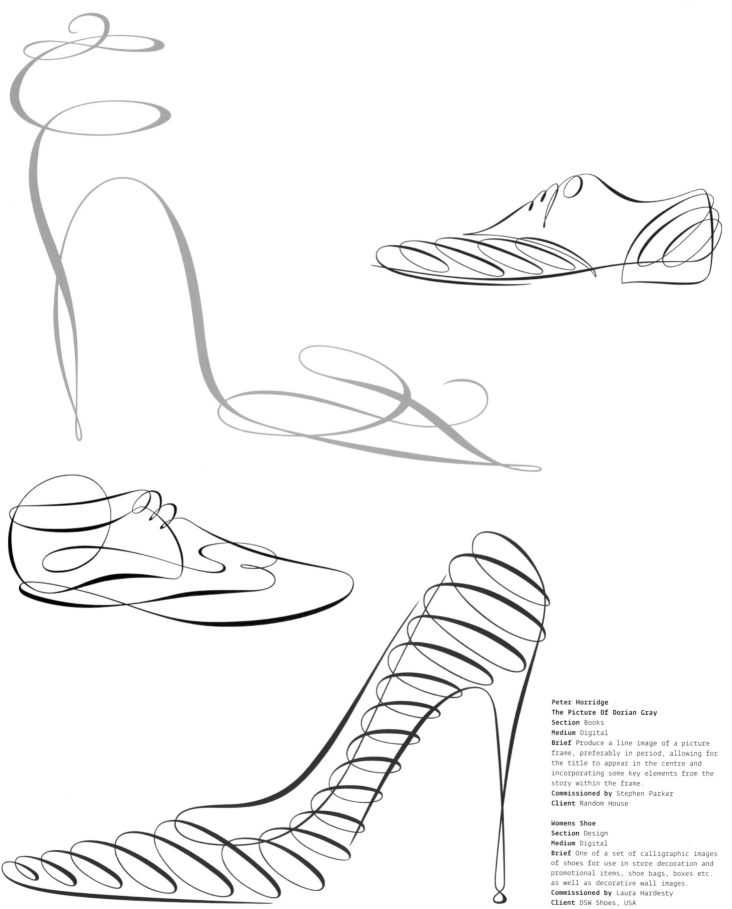

Peter Horridge /
The Picture Of Dorian Gray
Section Books
Medium Digital
Brief Produce a line image of a picture
frame, preferably in period, allowing for
the title to appear in the centre and
incorporating some key elements from the
story within the frame.
Commissioned by Stephen Parker
Client Random House

Womens Shoe
Section Design
Medium Digital
Brief One of a set of calligraphic images
of shoes for use in store decoration and
promotional items, shoe bags, boxes etc.
as well as decorative wall images.
Commissioned by Laura Hardesty
Client DSW Shoes, USA

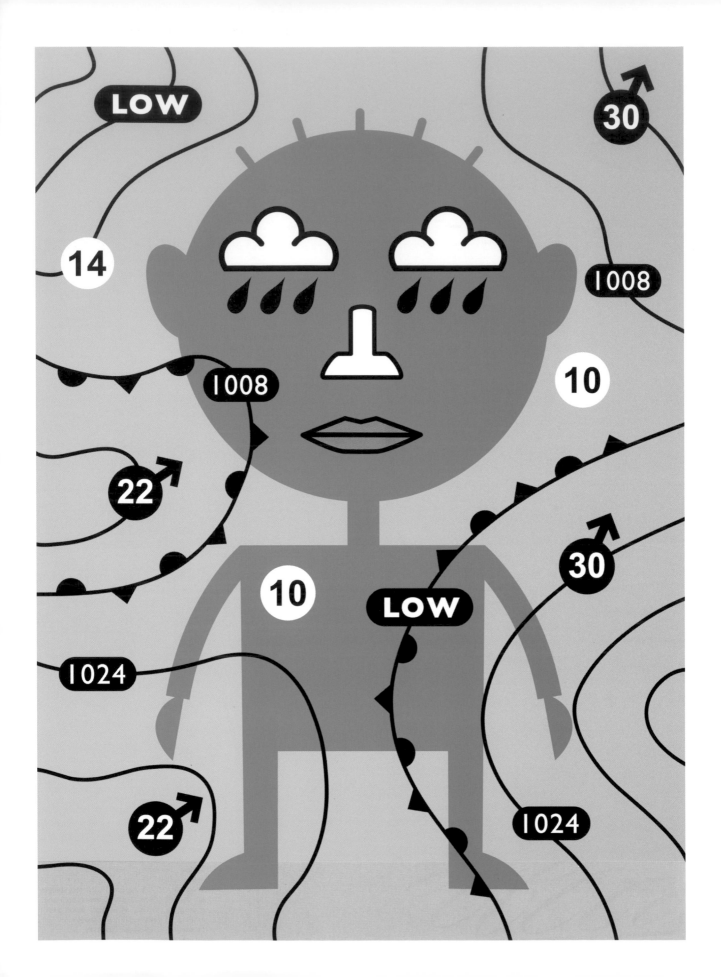

Patrick Hat /
Low
Section Self Promotion
Medium Digital
Brief To adapt the 'weather graphics'
into an illustration format.

Paul Blow /
Love Bites
Section Editorial
Medium Mixed media and digital
Brief Valentine's Day - If you're
planning a feast of amorous adventure,
you'll want your menu to push all the
right buttons. But do aphrodisiacs
actually work?
Commissioned by Stephen Petch
Client Independent News & Media

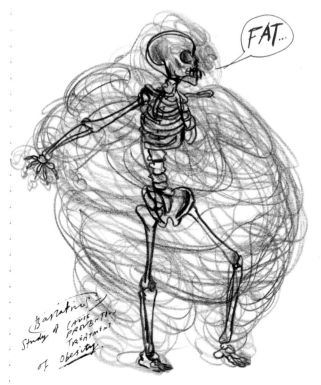

Simon Spilsbury
Rumour Flower
Section Editorial
Medium Mixed media
Brief To illustrate rumour.
Commissioned by Paul Davis
Client The Drawbridge

Fatty Fumes
Section Self Promotion
Medium Mixed media
Brief Content for publication on obesity.

Same Skeleton
Section Self Promotion
Medium Pencil
Brief Content for publication on obesity.

The Electoral Commission

IT ONLY TOOK ME A MOMENT TO REGISTER ☐

I MANAGED TO MISS THE MOMENT ☐

YOUR CHOICE. MAKE SURE NOTHING STOPS YOU VOTING.
REGISTER BY APRIL 16

0800 876 6444   londonelects.org.uk

The Electoral Commission

DON'T FORGET. LONDON ELECTIONS MAY 1

londonelects.org.uk

The Electoral Commission

I'M GOING TO LONDONELECTS.ORG.UK TO FIND OUT HOW TO VOTE ☐

I'M GOING ROUND IN CIRCLES ☐

YOUR CHOICE. MAKE SURE NOTHING STOPS YOU VOTING ON MAY 1

0800 876 6444   londonelects.org.uk

The Electoral Commission

I KNOW THE POLLS ARE OPEN 7AM TO 10PM ☐

THEY'RE BOUND TO BE OPEN AFTER THE PUB CLOSES ☐

YOUR CHOICE. MAKE SURE NOTHING STOPS YOU VOTING ON MAY 1

0800 876 6444   londonelects.org.uk

Simon Spilsbury /
Miss The Moment /
Bulb /
Circles /
Man In Glass
Section Advertising
Medium Mixed media
Brief Appeal to every demographic to
maximise votes in London mayoral elections.
Commissioned by
John Messum and Raymond Chan
Client Farm
Commissioned for
London Electoral Commission

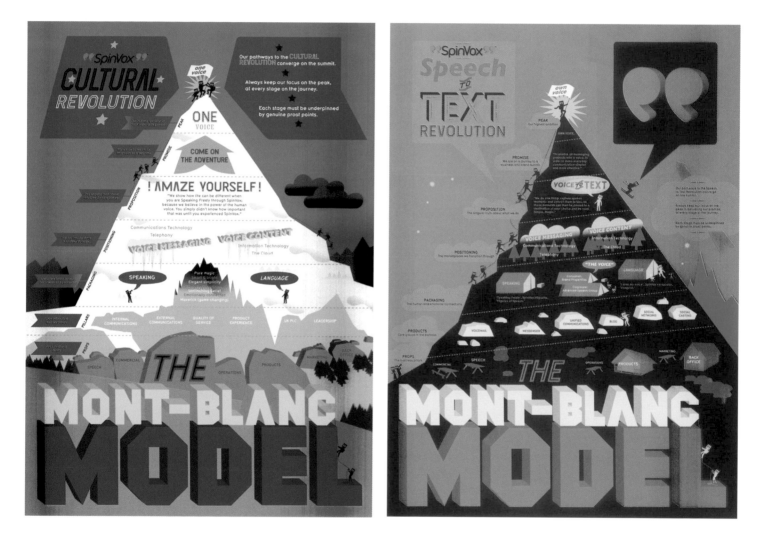

Andrew Baker /
SpinVox - Ice Cap / SpinVox - Mont Blanc
Section Design
Medium Digital
Brief To design an A1 image combining
elements of both classic poster design
and digital imagery to promote SpinVox's
key messages in-house.
Commissioned by Steve Wallington
Client Point Blank Collective
Commissioned for SpinVox

Lasse Skarbovik
Wall-painting
Section Design
Medium Digital
Brief Wallpainting for a media house
"Borgen" in Norway, 3 x 6 meter.
Commissioned by Kennet Hansen
Client Lovechild
Commissioned for Borgen

Top Ten IT Of The Year
Section Editorial
Medium Digital
Brief Top ten IT issues of the year.
Commissioned by Bernadette Gillen
Client CA magazaine

Tom Gaul /
Winehouse
Section Self Promotion
Medium Mixed
Brief Create an interesting visual idea
to promote my work & website.

The Amazing Ankle Bollocks Man
Section Editorial
Medium Mixed media
Brief All Ears section of the Guardian
Guide: Brief - To produce an illustration
based on an overheard conversation
between 2 gentlemen in a pub discussing a
sensitive health complaint described by
one of the men as feeling like 'pulling
my bollocks through my ankles!'.
Commissioned by Sara Ramsbottom
Client The Guardian Guide

Paul Cox
Upper Rock Gardens
Section Self Promotion
Medium Watercolour
Brief A personal piece.

St George's, Kemptown
Section Self Promotion
Medium Watercolour
Brief A personal piece.

Ashley Potter /
Concern
Section Books
Medium Acylic, gouache, digital
Brief Provide an image which depicts
one of the themes within the 3 stories.
The artist chose the uneasiness existing
between female and male lead characters
within each realtionship.
Commissioned by Anthony Caleshu
Client University of Plymouth Press
Commissioned for Short Fiction
- a visual, literary journal

Andy Potts /
Insight Track
Section Design
Medium Mixed media
Brief To illustrate a market research
timeline, including the relevant
historical surroundings.
Commissioned by Stephen Wake
Client Fortune Street
Commissioned for Esomar

The Disappearance Of Aju Iroaga
Section Editorial
Medium Digital
Brief Illustration for an article about
the mysterious disappearance of a
Candian forester.
Commissioned by Michel Rousseau
Client Readers Digest Canada

Getting To Know You
Section Books
Medium Digital
Brief To design a cover for a collection
of sci-fi short stories by David Marusek.
Commissioned by David Stevenson
Client Random House
Commissioned for
Getting To Know You by David Marusek

Legacy
Section New Media
Medium Digital animation
Brief Animated sequences to support a
film promoting High Speed 1 shown at the
Royal Opening Gala of St.Pancras Station,
November 2007.
Commissioned by Jim Owen, Ben Gallop
Client Brand & Deliver Creative
Commissioned for High Speed 1

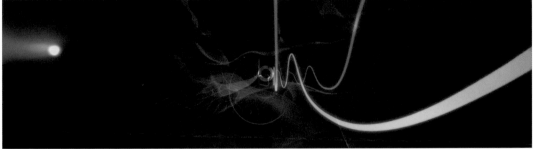

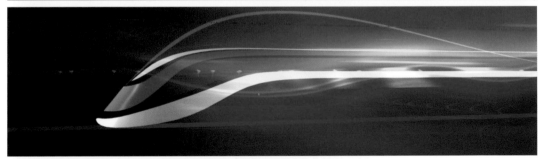

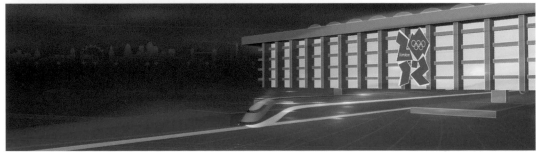

Posy

Linda Newbery & Catherine Rayner

Playful wrangler,

Knitting tangler.

Spider catcher,

Sofa scratcher.

Posy!

Catherine Rayner
Posy
Section Children's Books
Medium Ink and watercolour
Brief We wanted to match the simplicity
and beauty of the words with a classic,
clean design that showcased perfectly the
work of this exciting new artist, who is
also an exceptional draughtswoman.
Commissioned by Kate Burns
Client Orchard Books

She's a . . .

Stephen Collins
Ding Dong
Section Editorial
Medium Pencil rough, Photoshop colouring
Brief The Day Job - weekly Cartoon in Career, The Times.
Commissioned by Carol Lewis
Client The Times

Procrastination Pays
Section Editorial
Medium Pencil Rough, Photoshop colouring
Brief The Day Job: a weekly Strip in the Career section of The Times.
Commissioned by Carol Lewis
Client The Times

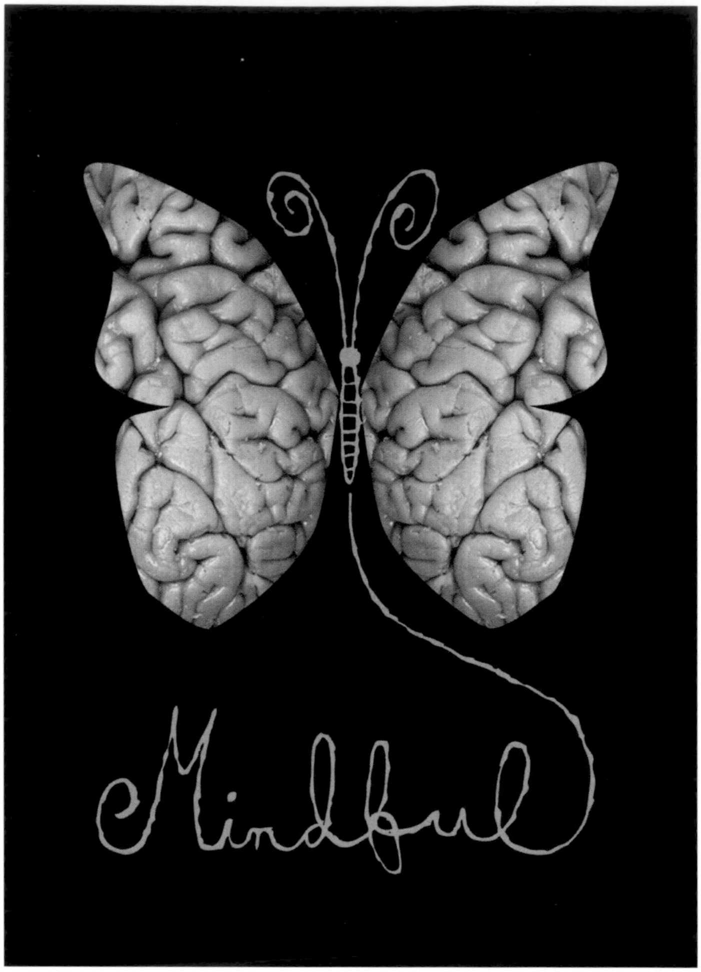

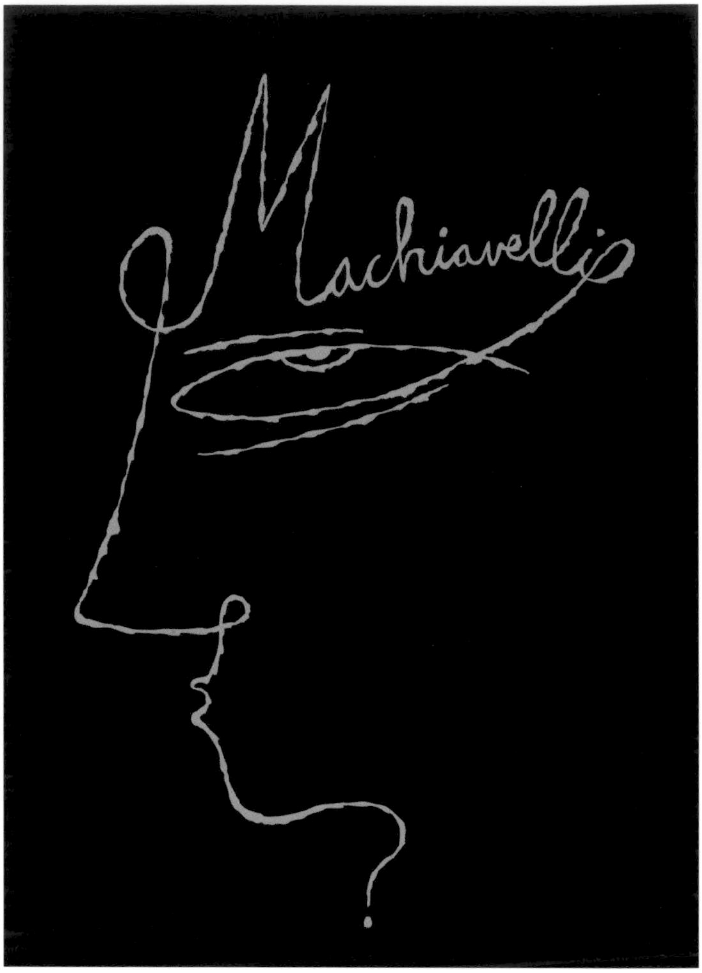

Kenneth Andersson /
Mindful / Machiavelli!
Section Self Promotion
Medium Ink and digital
Brief About management.

Bläckis
Section Books
Medium Ink and digital
Brief Illustrate chapter 9 about agents
in "The Illustrator's Guide to Law and
Business Practice".
Commissioned by Derek Brazell
Client Association of Illustrators

Food!
Section Self Promotion
Medium Ink and digital
Brief Food!

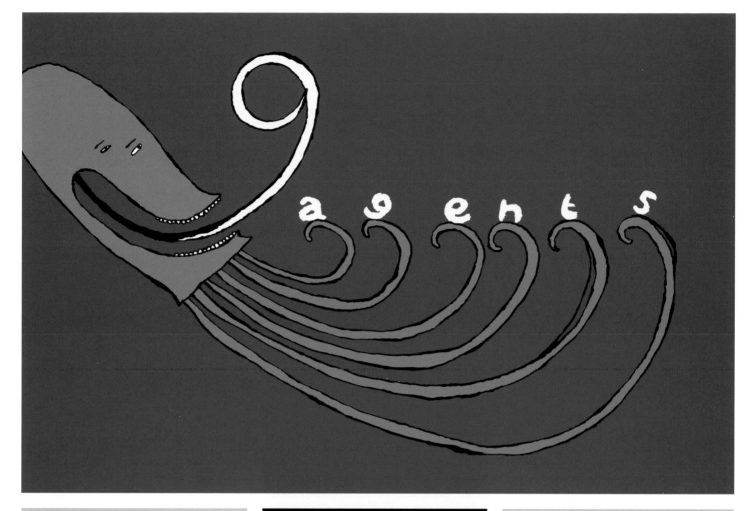

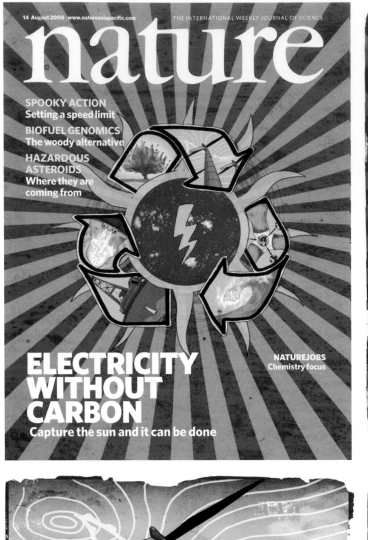

Jay Taylor /
Alternative Energy /
Geothermal /
Wind Power /
Wave Power
Section Editorial
Medium Mixed media
Brief Create a bold iconic imagery for
magazine feature and cover.
Commissioned by Barbara Izbebska
Client Macmillan
Commissioned for Nature magazine

Dominic Clubb /
Shoe Hell
Section Self Promotion
Medium digital
Brief This is a humorous illustration
showing what hell would be like for
a shoe.

Paul Wearing /
Acute Care For Sick Children
Section Advertising
Medium Digital
Brief Illustration for fundraising book,
highlighting the work the hospital does in
caring for acutely sick children.
Commissioned by Doug Joseph
Client Douglas Joseph Partners
Commissioned for Cedars Sinai Medical Center

The Return
Section Self Promotion
Medium Digital
Brief Limited Edition
print developed for Illustrative Berlin.

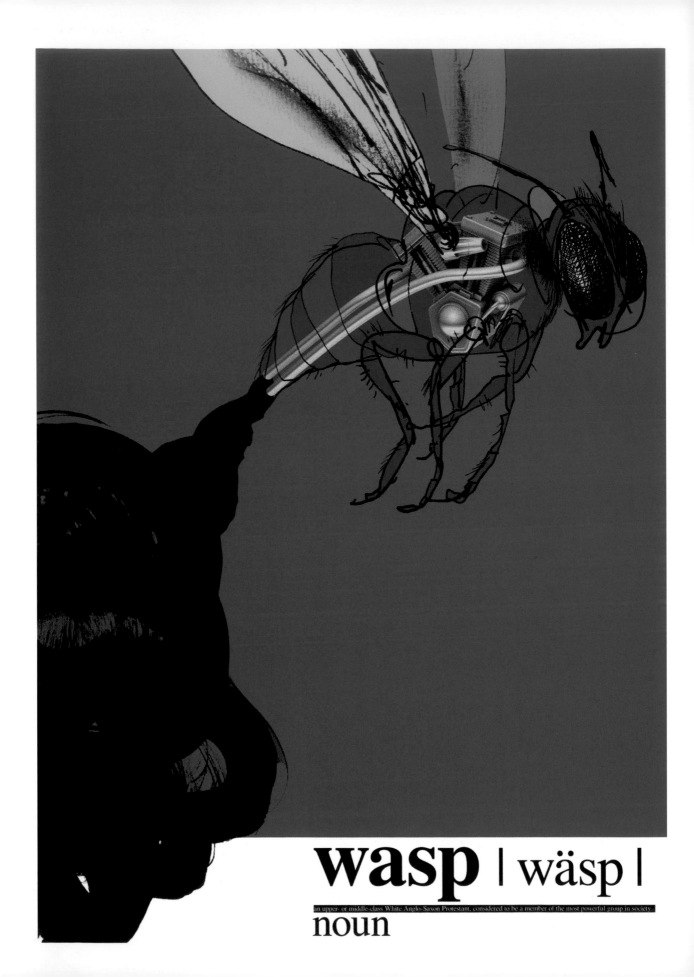

wasp | wäsp |

an upper- or middle-class White Anglo-Saxon Protestant, considered to be a member of the most powerful group in society.

noun

Artbombers /
Wasp
Section Self Promotion
Medium Mixed media
Brief Content for Artbombers publication 1.

Fan
Section Self Promotion
Medium Mixed media
Brief Content for Artbombers publication 1.

Spider
Section Self Promotion
Medium Mixed media
Brief Content for Artbombers publication 1.

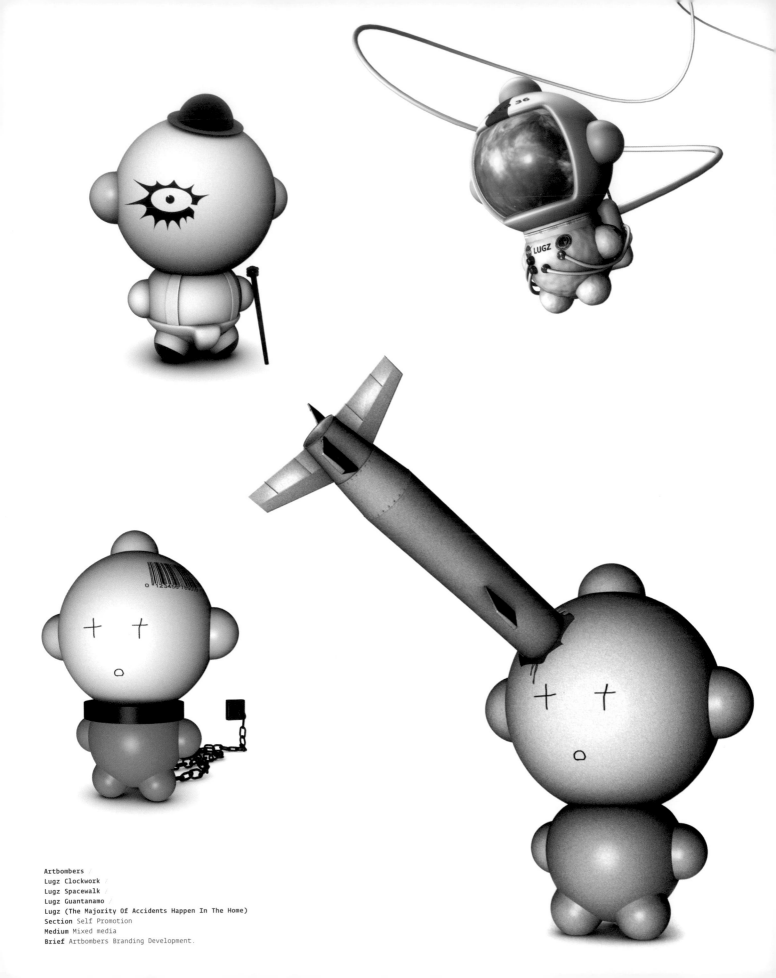

Artbombers /
Lugz Clockwork /
Lugz Spacewalk /
Lugz Guantanamo /
Lugz (The Majority Of Accidents Happen In The Home)
Section Self Promotion
Medium Mixed media
Brief Artbombers Branding Development.

David Convey
Bra Bra
Section Self Promotion
Medium Pen and Mac
Brief Personal experimental work - create
a funny image for self promotion.

Suzanne Duffy /
Cityscape 1: Resident's Summary
Section Self Promotion
Medium Digital
Brief A visual description of
observations from an urban habitat.

Urban Bird Illustrated Lightpillars
Section Self Promotion
Medium Digital
Brief A visual description of
observations from an urban habitat.

Oliver Hydes
Attempting To Walk
Through The Lanes On
A Saturday
Section Books
Medium Pen and digital
Brief To Illustrate a
particular moment that is
personal and relevant to
Brighton to be printed
in a Black & White
book published for the
Brighton Festival.
Commissioned by
Lawrence Zeegen,
Adrian Driscoll
Client
UnmadeUp Publishing
Commissioned for
The Brighton Festival

CHOICES

CITIES

DEMAND

RESOURCES

Anchors

ELECTRICITY

ENVIRONMENT

MOBILITY

DEMOGRAPHY

TECHNOLOGY

Shell energy scenarios

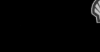

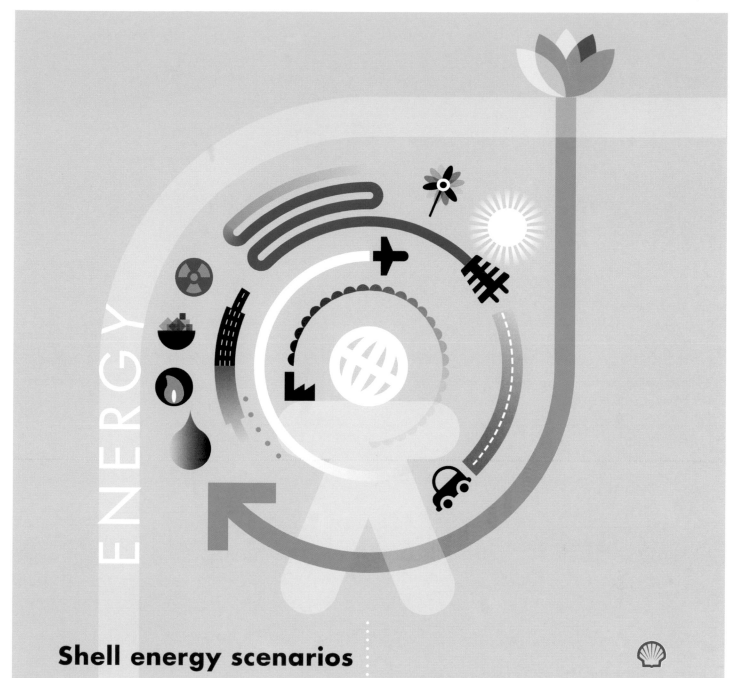

ENERGY

Shell energy scenarios

Peter Grundy /
Shell Energy Scenarios Anchors Poster
Section Design
Medium Digital
Brief Create a system of images showing
energy topics.
Commissioned by Shirley Wright
Client Shell International
Commissioned for
Shell Energy Scenarios campaign

Shell Energy Scenarios Poster
Section Design
Medium Digital
Brief Design/illustrate a poster for a
conference on energy.
Commissioned by Shirley Wright
Client Shell International
Commissioned for
Shell Energy Scenarios campaign

>>
Chips With Everything
Section Design
Medium Digital
Brief An illustration showing things that
have 'chips' in them.
Commissioned by John Towell
Client Luminous
Commissioned for ARM International

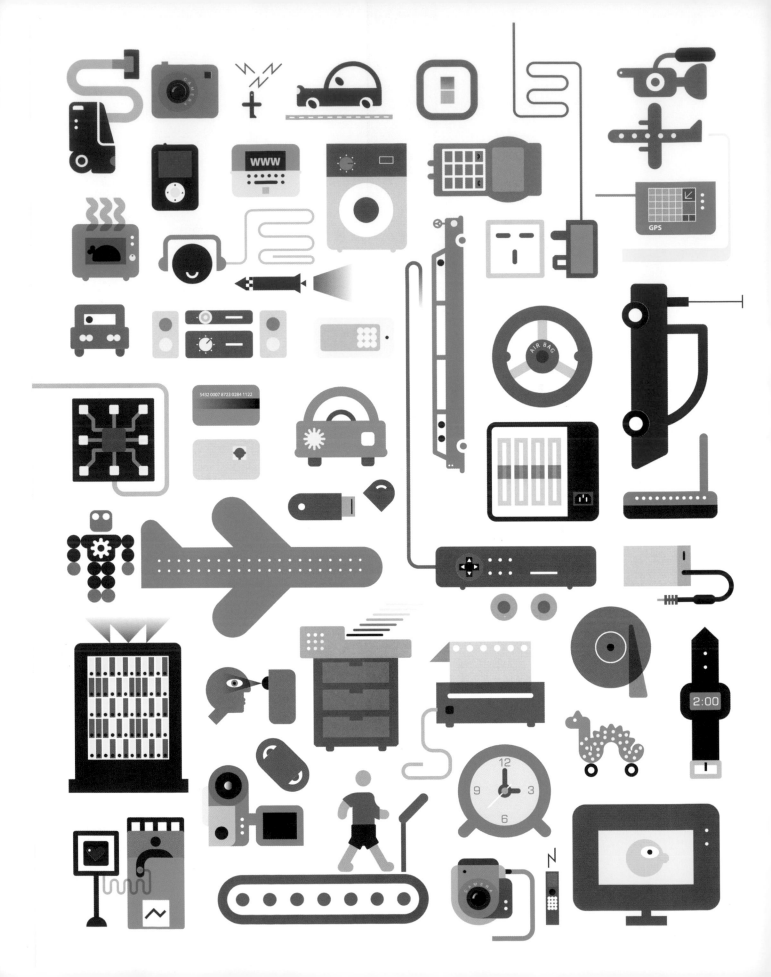

Max Ellis /
Bill Bailey Website
Section New Media
Medium Digital
Brief A completely open brief to produce
a wondrous web site for the comedian Bill
Bailey. Only the function and number
of rooms was specified, ie Shop, Tour,
navigation page, news etc. I tried to
rethink the nature of how each section
would be approached so that it would be
an entertaining and expanding journey
through Bills mind.
Commissioned by
Bill and Kris Bailey, Richard Hudson
Client Bill Bailey and Vanilla Storm

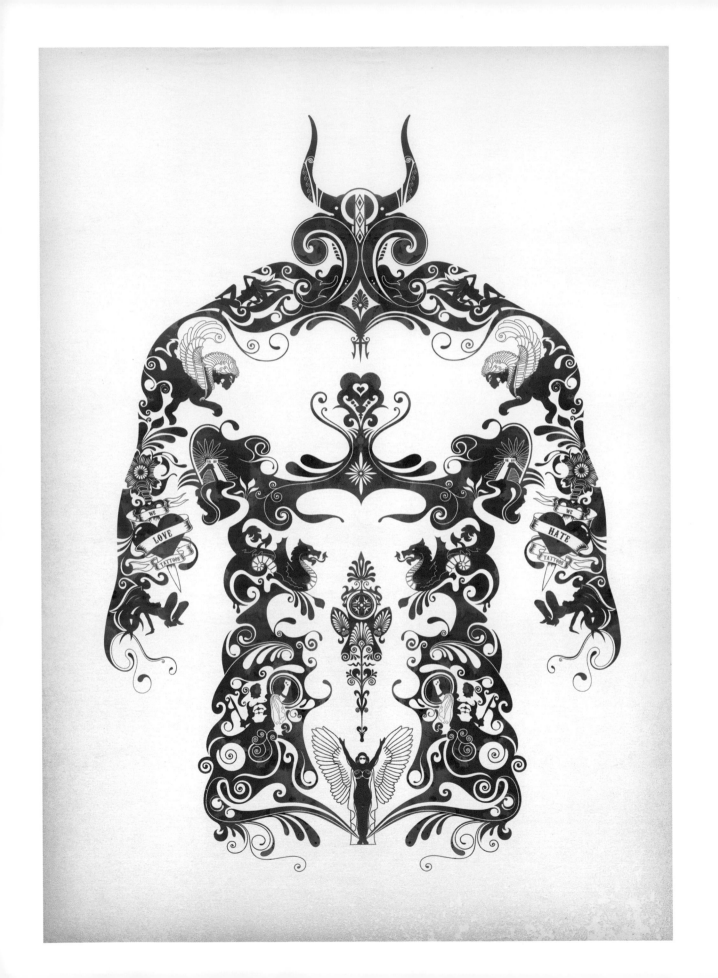

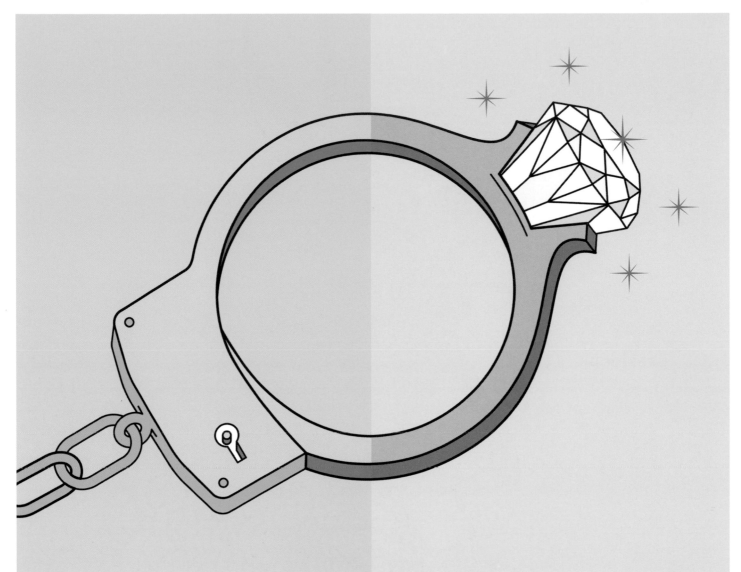

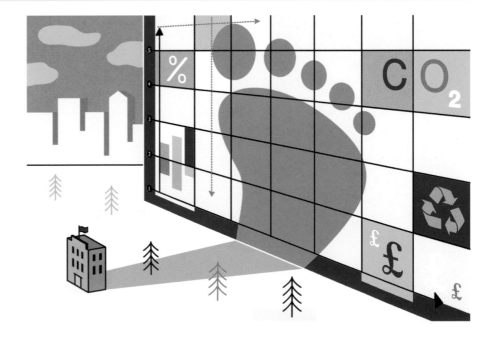

Tom Lane /
Extrovert
Section Self Promotion
Medium Digitally drawn artwork
Brief To create a delicate, striking,
tattoo referenced piece that plays with
our perception of form. I choose to look
at the the male torso in a new way.

Cyrus Deboo /
No Tie-Ups No Tie-Downs
Section Advertising
Medium Digital
Brief To illustrate the play on the
words 'No tie-ups No tie-downs' for
mobile broadband.
Commissioned by
Paul Paterson and Andrew Pogson
Client Lida
Commissioned for Vodafone

Carbon Footprint
Section Editorial
Medium Digital
Brief To illustrate an article about
how small businesses can measure their
carbon footprint.
Commissioned by Erroll Jones
Client Caspian Publishing
Commissioned for Real Business

Alison Haines /
Flying Fox
Section Self Promotion
Medium Pen and ink, computer aided design
Brief Original pen and ink drawing,
then made into print and a painting.
Self promotion.

Fitch:
Michelle Banister, Phill Rees, Cyan Koo
Inherently Kenyan
Section Design
Medium
Digital wallpaper and vinyl application
Brief To create some ambient colour coded wayfinding graphics which capture the true spirit of the culture of Kenya and the people of Kenya.
Client Safaricom Kenya

Alex T Smith /
Bella & Monty
Section Children's Books
Medium Digital
Brief Picture book written and
illustrated by Alex. Monty, the
cat is frightened of everything,
especially the dark. Bella, the dog
is fearless. She shows Monty that
things are not as scary as they seem.
Commissioned by Alison Still
Client Hodder Children's Books

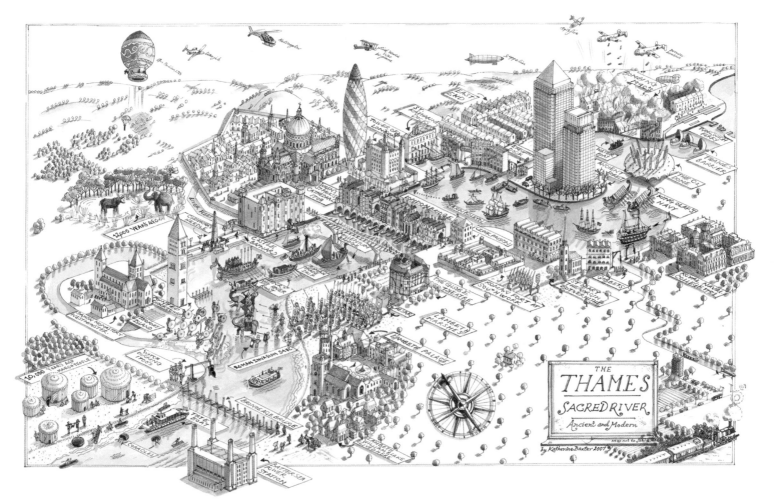

Katherine Baxter /
The Sacred River
(The History Of The Thames)
Section Editorial
Medium Pen, ink and watercolour
Brief A pull out poster for the launch of
Peter Ackroyd's book 'The Sacred River'
the history of the Thames. For the Book
section of the Saturday Times.
Commissioned by David Driver
Client Times Newspaper

Delphine Lebourgeois /
One Hundred Years Of Solitude
Section Self Promotion
Medium Mixed media
Brief Self Promotional book cover for
the novel by Gabriel Garcia Marquez.

Photo De Classe
Section Self Promotion
Medium Mixed media
Brief Personal piece, part of the
"Amazons" series and illustrating
the idea of "competition".

Danny Allison /
Obsessive Compulsive Disorders "Sharks"
Section Editorial
Medium Photography, spray paint, oil
pastel, ink, collage, pencil, chalk
Brief To illustrate a young girls
unfortunate disorder of being afraid of
water in any form. Water would set off
panic and this made it impossible for her
to have a bath or shower.
Commissioned by name
Client Subterfuge magazine

it is easy to day dream when the days get darker

Zara Wood
Woody For Topshop: Star Gaze
Section Design
Medium Digital drawings
Brief To create a theme and illustrations for a limited edition 8 piece capsule collection for Topshop.
Commissioned by Charlotte Henson
Client Topshop

Daniel Pudles
Waves Of Pleasure
Section Editorial
Medium Mixed media
Brief Book review of "Breath" by Tim Winton. A coming of age and surfing tale.
Commissioned by Carole Alimo
Client The Economist

China Syndrome
Section Editorial
Medium Mixed media
Brief Book review on new thrillers using China as a backdrop.
Commissioned by Suzy Connolly
Client The Economist

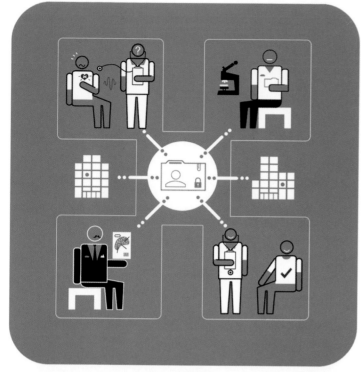

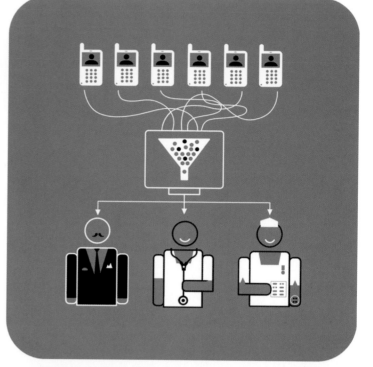

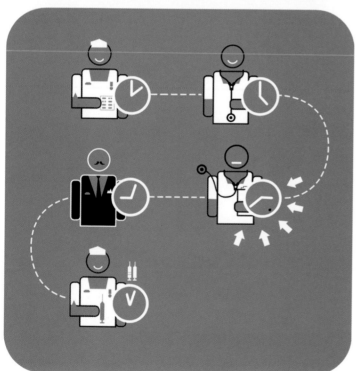

Ian Whadcock /
Growing Pains
Section Editorial
Medium Digital
Brief To accompany feature on the need
for small businesses to expand and grow
over time and how this can be achieved -
by franchise / by region / by network.
Commissioned by Gary Hill / Nick Dixon
Client Caspian
Commissioned for Real Business Magazine

Clinical Solutions
Section Design
Medium Digital
Brief To develop a simple flexible
language for use across a range of
brochures - clinical management software
solutions for healthcare professionals
(22 drawings overall) 4 entered.
Commissioned by Ed Williams
Client Williams & Crosby
Commissioned for Clinical Solutions

Ian Whadcock
Flight
Section Design
Medium Digital
Brief To re-interpret the word 'flight' as part of a
brochure to announce the re-naming of Manchester School
of Art summer 08. The brief Flight was derived from an
original Walter Crane drawing found at the University
building where he used to teach.
Commissioned by Dave Crow (Dean)
Client MMU
Commissioned for Manchester School of Art

Speed Writing
Section Editorial
Medium Digital
Brief Improbable Research - Philip M Parker is the
world's fastest book author, and given that he has been
at it only for about five years and already has more
than 85,000 books to his name, he is also probably the
most prolific.
Commissioned by John-Henry Barac
Client The Guardian Newspaper

Short Term Business Finance
Section Editorial
Medium Digital
Brief To accompany feature for B2B newspaper, which
deals with mortgage and banking industry news. This
piece looks at the need for short term finance and how
you can secure loans to avoid problems with cash flow.
Commissioned by Andra Roig
Client Source Media
Commissioned for Origination News

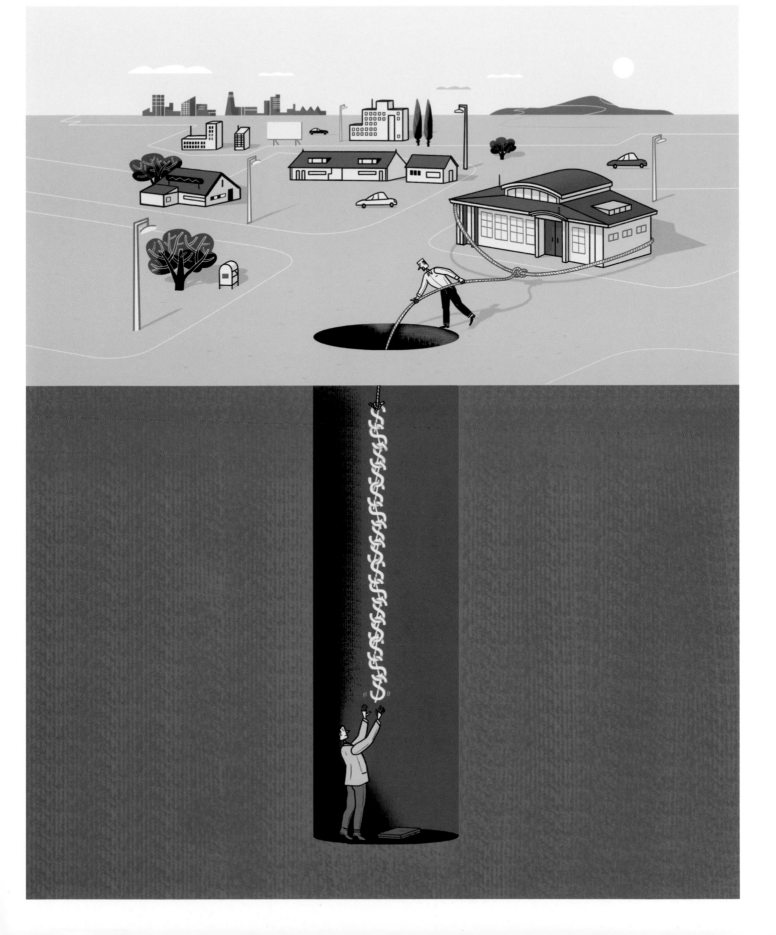

Paul Thurlby /
England
Section Self Promotion
Medium Digital
Brief Portraits of three of the current
England football team and their manager
Fabio Capello. Trying to get across their
individual personalities.

Victoria Ball /
That Yucky Love Thing
Section Children's Books
Medium
Acrylic and image transfer on paper
Brief Create original complimentary
illustrations for a 32-page picture book
for the 3-5 age group.
Commissioned by Paula Burgess
Client Gullane Children's Books

  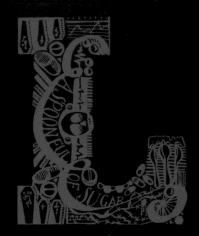

is for Horror,
poisonous ground.

is for atmosphere,
polluted, unsound.

is for Levels,
too high, make you sick.

is for Lifestyle,
a concept, a trick.

'O' is for on,
all the time,
Standby!

'W's waste,
filling ground,
piling high.

An 'E' for emissions,
nought out of ten.

Another for energy...
will run out—
what then?

is for new,
do you need it?
Do you?

Sarah Coleman /
Hallowe'en
Section Self Promotion
Medium Ink, digital and Flash
Brief An exhibition piece, animation
and Hallowe'en promo. A poem about my
environmental (and very scary) concerns
and a detailed illustrated letter for
each line.

Sainsbury's / Corns / Cough / Eyes / Warts
Section Advertising
Medium Inks
Brief Old fashioned service with thoroughly
modern medicine!
Commissioned by Rita Jugessur
Client Associated in Advertising Ltd.
Commissioned for Sainsbury's Pharmacy

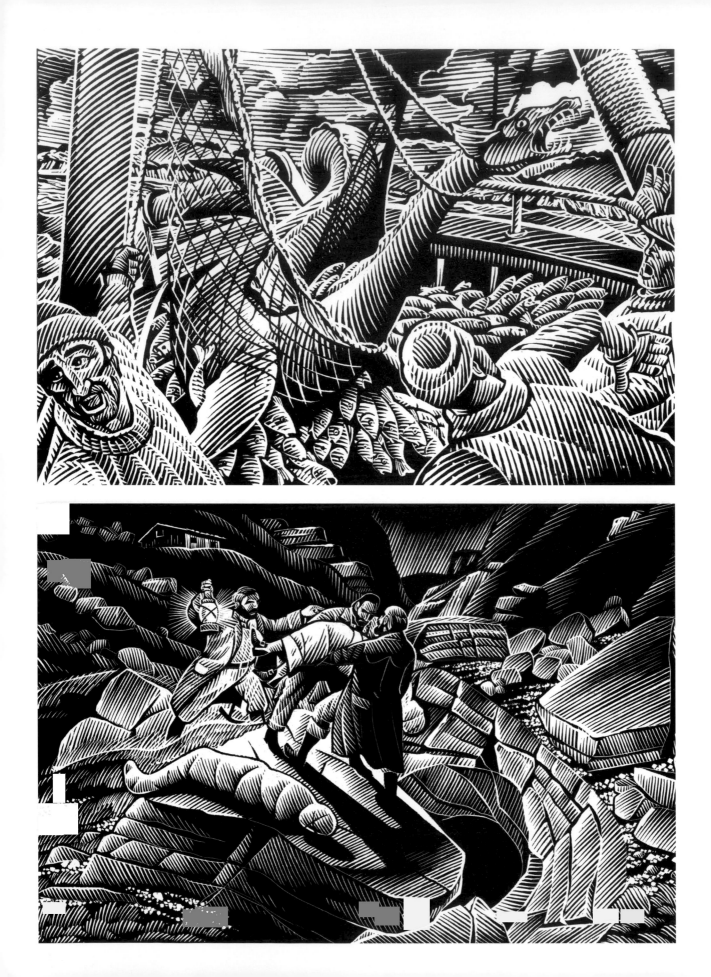

Pete Brewster
Mawgr / Murderous
Section Editorial
Medium Scraperboard
Brief Illustrating a feature of
ghostly stories.
Commissioned by Tim Bates
Client BBC Magazines

Greg McLeod
Skittles
Section Advertising
Medium Charcoal on paper
Brief To create a series on characters
and layouts in a rough and edgy style fit
for a 18-35 audience.
Commissioned by Heather Wright
Client Aardman
Commissioned for Mars/TBWA

Matthew Richardson /
Kasabian In Full Flight
Section Advertising
Medium Mixed and digital
Brief To create an image that would
work in various formats and sizes
for a billboard advertising campaign
showing the 'Liveness' of the band
Kasabian, to promote the Vodafone Live
Music Awards on Channel 4.
Commissioned by Chris Felstead
Client BBH
Commissioned for Vodafone

Ian Pollock
David And Goliath
Section Editorial
Medium Watercolour, ink and gouache
Brief Big banks being threatened by
small banks.
Commissioned by David Twardawa
Client Caspian Publishing
Commissioned for Real Deals Magazine

Two Blind Men Cured
Section Self Promotion
Medium Ink
Brief One of an ongoing lifetimes work
"The Miracles of Christ".

T.S Spookytooth
Fearless Flynn And Other Tales
Section Children's Books
Medium Acrylic
Brief To illustrate the story of Fearless Flynn
who does battle with three scary skeletons.
Commissioned by Nikki Kenwood
Client HarperCollins

Rory Willis
Mark E Smith As Ringmaster
Section Advertising
Medium Digital
Brief Produce a dadaist style image of
Mark E Smith and The Fall to be used as
part of advertising for the upcoming tour.
Commissioned by Florian Zumfelde
Client Florian Zumfelde Design Studio
Commissioned for MT World

der
Zirkusdirektor

20⁶

Mark E Smith as
The Ringmaster

Bob Venables
The Intrepid Hunters Widen Their Search
Searching For Bond Profits
Section Advertising
Medium Oils
Brief To produce an illustration as part of
the series Artemis the Profit Hunter who
has the ability to go to great lengths to
discover great profits.
Commissioned by Russel Wailes
Client RPM3 Beechwood
Commissioned for Artemis

Mei Matsuoka
Footprints In The Snow
Section Children's Books
Medium Mixed media
Brief To write and to illustrate a
picture book for children - age range
aprox. 4-8 years.
Commissioned by Rona Selby
Client Andersen Press Ltd

Petra Stefankova /
Summer In Paris And Prague /
Summer In London And Tokyo
Section Self Promotion
Medium Digital
Brief What is summer?

Don't Wake Me Up /
How To Blow
Section Editorial
Medium Photoshop and Illustrator
Brief How to Blow.
Commissioned by Maggie Murphy
Client The Guardian Weekend

Sleeping Rabbit
Section Self Promotion
Medium Vector illustration -
Photoshop & Illustrator
Brief None - personal work.

Beck Wheeler
I Heart NY
Section Self Promotion
Medium digital
Brief To create a character illustration for
a deck of 'mixie' cards, which were part of
The Jacky Winter Group promotional campaign
for the Icon5 conference in New York. Each
of the 26 illustrators involved designed a
character that could be cut into 3 parts, a
head, a body and legs. These cards could be
shuffled and rearranged to create different
combinations of characters.

Steve Simpson
Fifteen
Section Design
Medium Pen, ink and digital
Brief For a 700 page book celebrating
Red Dog Design's 15th birthday. Depict
the process through your relationship
with Red Dog Design Consultants and cross
reference your concept with the number 15
in some way.
Commissioned by Mary Doherty
Client Red Dog Design Consultants

Mr Brown From Irvinestown
Section Books
Medium Pencil and digital
Brief To illustrate the poem: Mr. Brown
from Irvinestown greets the chickens
with a frown. He eats chicken soup on
top of their coop, dressed in his wife's
wedding gown.
Commissioned by Henry Muldrow
Client Stichting Culturele Droomwevers

Richard Johnson
Fabulously Feathered Flip Flappers
Section Children's Books
Medium Acrylic
Brief To illustrate my own story, 'My Grandpa's Amazing Inventions'. This spread shows Grandpa and his Granddaughter flying with the help of some 'Fabulously Feathered Flip Flappers'.
Commissioned by Mike Jolley
Client Templar Publishing
Commissioned for
My Grandpa's Amazing Inventions

The Genie Of The Lamp
Section Children's Books
Medium Acrylic
Brief To illustrate the story of Aladdin. The image should show the Genie of the Lamp being summoned by a surprised Aladdin, it will also be used as a jigsaw puzzle within the book.
Commissioned by Kayt Manson
Client Pan MacMillan
Commissioned for Aladdin Jigsaw Book

**The Miserable Magician And
The Forest Flood**
Section Self Promotion
Medium Acrylic
Brief Develop some of my sketch book characters, locations and drawings into more finished pieces to help illustrate some of my stories for children.

**The Great And Magnificent Creature
Catcher And Dim The Robot Mark 2**
Section Self Promotion
Medium Acrylic and mixed media
Brief Develop some of my sketch book characters, locations and drawings into more finished pieces to help illustrate some of my stories for children.

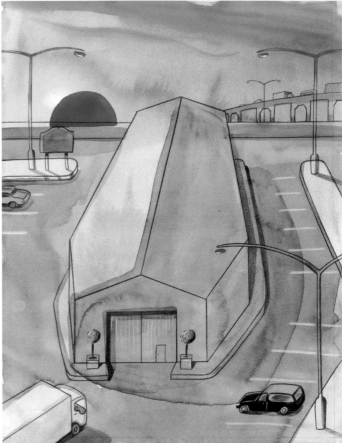

Noma Bar
Clash Of The Titles
Section Editorial
Medium Digital
Brief You've bought your plot and built
your property, so what happens when
somebody else claims they owned the
land all along? Undisputed ownership
of land is the number one concern for
international developers.
Commissioned by Tina Smith
Client CMP Information Ltd
Commissioned for Property Week Global

Toby Morison
Sheds Of Death
Section Editorial
Medium Pastel
Brief After a large disaster, there
will have to be somewhere to store the
accumulated corpses. The drawing says
everything that words couldn't.
Commissioned by Richard Krzyzak
Client CMP information Ltd
Commissioned for Property Week

Vicky Newman /
Red Peacock
Section Self Promotion
Medium Hand drawn line and digital colour
Brief This illustration was a self promotional piece looking to explore the theme of East meets West using a rich colour palette and hand drawn line work.

Jonas Bergstrand
Virgin Atlantic Pitch
Section Self Promotion
Medium Digital, Photoshop and Illustrator
Brief Style test images for a Virgin
Atlantic campaign. Artwork was not used
in the end.

James Greenway /
In Bloom
Section Self Promotion
Medium Digital Print
Brief Self motivated project to
capture the concept of thoughts
and ideas blossoming from my mind.

Oliver Jeffers /
The Great Paper Caper
Section Children's Books
Medium Mixed media
Brief To create a Picture Book suitable
for HarperCollins first full colour
publication on FSC paper.
Client HarperCollins
Commissioned by
Sue Buswell and Amanda Riddout

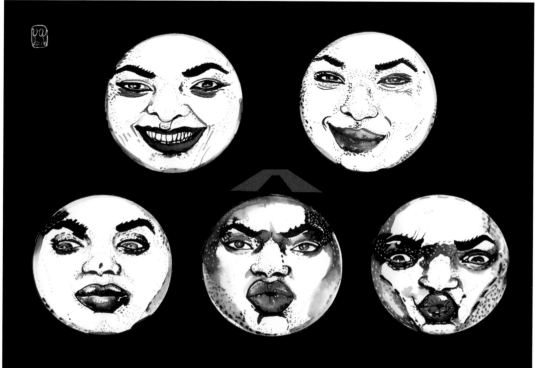

Valérie Pézeron
Le Ruffiant
Section New Media
Medium Mixed media and music video
Brief I was asked to create a background to
accompany the edgy music video Le Ruffiant
by video artist Drak.
Commissioned by Jimmy Tidey
Client TheThingIs

Moon Elements
Section New Media
Medium Quink ink and pen, wash and digital
Brief Elements for a 2D animation for France
Ô cable TV short logo trailer or ident.
Commissioned by
Walles Kotra and Corinne Alexia
Client France Télévisions
Commissioned for France Ô

Garry Parsons
Positive Power
Section Editorial
Medium Digital
Brief A positive approach to care by nurses
makes all the difference to a patients'
hospital experience.
Commissioned by Minesh Parmar
Client RCN Publishing
Commissioned for Nursing Standard Magazine

Win The Cold War
Section Editorial
Medium Digital
Brief Tips to keep your immune system
firing on cold winter runs.
Commissioned by Russell Fairbrother
Client Natmag-Rodale
Commissioned for Runner's World Magazine

Innocent Bystanders?
Section Editorial
Medium Digital
Brief Should you intervene when you see a
work colleague being victimised?
Commissioned by Roger Browning
Client The Guardian

Simon Pemberton
Paradise Lost
Section Editorial
Medium Mixed media
Brief To create a dramatic cover image to
show the banking community's fall from
grace as the world credit crunch deepens.
Client The Economist cover

Section Design
Medium Mixed media
Panama La Esmeralda
Brief To create an rich, atmospheric
Panamanian coastal scene to reflect the
nature of this coffee blend and show
the environment in which it is grown.
Java Jampit
Brief To capture the feel of the hot
lava fields of Indonesia to reflect the
dark flavour of this coffee grown on
volcanic soil.
Zambia Terranova
Brief To show the landscape of the
Terranova estate in Zambia where this
coffee is grown reflecting "its dark,
fruity full bodied nature".
Organic Nicaragua Matagalpa
Brief To capture the feel of this
rich, organically grown coffee and the
landscape and soils where it is grown.
Client Pearl Fisher
Commissioned for Taylors of Harrogate

Simon Pemberton
Rime Of The Ancient Mariner
Section Books
Medium Mixed media
Brief "The dead men stood together,
for a charnel-dungeon fitter, all
fixed on me their stony eyes, that in
the moon did glitter".
Commissioned by
Darrel Rees and Helen Osborne
Client Heart

Partners In Crime
Section Editorial
Medium Mixed media
Brief An apparently honest Russian
in military uniform offers you a
fantastically lucrative opportunity to
build a glitzy development in central
Moscow. All he needs is a few million
dollars upfront. Too good to be true?
Commissioned by Tina Smith
Client CMP Information Ltd
Commissioned for Property Week global

Tolu Shofule
Moses And The Princess
Section New Media
Medium Photoshop
Brief To illustrate the Biblical Story of Moses.
Commissioned by Olu Ojuroye
Client Virtue Interactive Productions

Bill Sanderson /
The Voyage Of The Demeter
Section Editorial
Medium Ccraperboard
Brief Depicting the arrival of the
schooner, bringing Dracula to Whitby.
Commissioned by Hazel Brown
Client BBC Worldwide
Commissioned for Radio Times

Sarah Lippett
My Year In Lists
Death To Los Campesinos!
Poster Art For Los Campesinos!
Hold On Now, Youngster...
Section Design
Medium Ink and Photoshop
Brief To design the band's album, singles and poster.
Commissioned by Los Campesinos!
Client Los Campesinos!

Rosemary Squire
Real Meat And Two Veg
Section Self Promotion
Medium Polymer clay and found objects
Brief To create a series of illustrations
highlighting recent food/eating campaigns
by celebrity chefs.

Annie West /
**After Years At Sea, Columbus Finally
Discovers The New World**
Section Self Promotion
Medium Pen and ink
Brief Part of a series examining moments
in history. Used as part of
an exhibition.

Chris Vine
Maypole On The Mersey
Section Design
Medium Acrylic
Brief An image to represent an aspect of
Liverpool's history and culture for the
2008 celebrations. Ferries have crossed
the River Mersey for over 1,000 years.
Commissioned by Alex Corina
Client Artworks Liverpool

Food Map Of Ireland
Section Editorial
Medium Ink and watercolour
Brief A map of Ireland showing regional
food and drink. This image supported
a series of articles describing Irish
culinary history.
Commissioned by Roger Standen
Client Design Dimension
Commissioned for Cook School Magazine

Pond Life
Section Self Promotion
Medium Acrylic
Brief Mass tourism between the bulrushes,
oil-rigs among the lily pads, aeroplanes
chasing dragonflies - a typical day in
the life of a suburban garden pond.

Caroline Church
Mediterranean Landscape
Section Advertising
Medium Scraperboard
Brief Brief was to do an image that could be cropped randomly and used as a background 'wallpaper' for packaging a range of different foods. Client wanted something vague that didn't look like it represented anywhere in particular or showed any specific food.
Commissioned by Lisa Gomm
Client Satellite Creative
Commissioned for La Fresca

Buell Motorbike
Section Editorial
Medium Scraperboard
Brief Brief was to produce a medieval scene of a Buell motorbike about to be burnt at the stake. The ad line was "It's not easy to be ahead of your time".
Commissioned by Isabelle
Client Euro RSCG
Commissioned for Buell

Carolyn King /
The Navigator
Section Self Promotion
Medium Life sized hand cut mirror mosaic
Brief The camel reflects a world when
survival truly depended on environment.
It partners my children's story (with
line illustrations) for use in an
educational context.

Rod Hunt
Torpedo Volume Two
Section Books
Medium Digital
Brief Create a cover for Volume Two of
Torpedo Fiction Quarterly, reflecting a
wild west theme.
Commissioned by Chris Flynn
Client Falcon vs Monkey, Falcon Wins

1st Byte Virtual Tour
Section New Media
Medium Digital
Brief Create a fun & accurate
representation of digital printer 1st
Byte's headquarters to be animated as
an interactive virtual tour website to
promote the company's services.
Commissioned by Jamie Sergent
Client Strange
Commissioned for
1st Byte digital printers

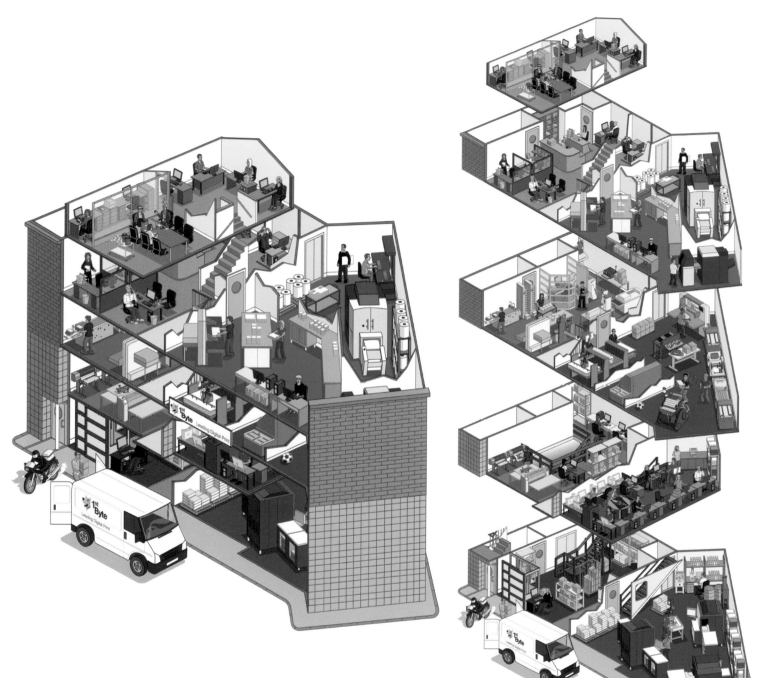

Claudia Boldt
UUGGHH!
Section Self Promotion
Medium Mixed media
Brief UUGGHH! is a book
about self-esteem, the fear
of fitting in, and the
overvaluing of appearance.

Marcus Irwin /
Panic On The Streets Of England
Section Self Promotion
Medium Screenprint
Brief Self-published limited edition
screenprint, created in response to the
rising levels of knife crime in the UK
during the year 2008.

Christopher Corr /
The Mandarins By Simone De Beauvoir
Section Books
Medium Gouaches on paper
Brief To illustrate Simone de Beauvoir's
novel The Mandarins: a book about life
in Paris for a group of intellectuals,
their love affairs and their plans for
the future.
Commissioned by Sheri Gee
Client The Folio Society

Deer & Birds
Section Self Promotion
Medium Gouaches on paper
Brief I wanted to create a joyful
and colourful impression of Christmas
and Winter. An image showing peace
and harmony.

Paul Holland
Dirty Rotter
Section Editorial
Medium Pencil, crayon, gouache, Photoshop
Brief Fashion Couture Week - celebrity
meets couture.
Commissioned by
via - Illustration Ltd (agent)
Client Fashion Monitor July 08

J'adore
Section Self Promotion
Medium Pencil, crayon, gouache, Photoshop
Brief Portrait of the French music/
performance artist Philippe Katerine,
famous for his song entitled -
'Louxor J'adore'.

Darren Diss /
Web Happy Hotelier
Section Editorial
Medium Mixed
Brief Show a hotelier who is
comfortable producing web promotion
for his business.
Commissioned by Joe McAllister
Client
William Reed Business Media Ltd
Commissioned for
H - The Hotel Magazine

ALL WORK AND NO PLAY
MAKES JACK A DULL BOY

John Miers /
Illumination
Section Self Promotion
Medium Digital
Brief What is illustration?

David Humphries /
All Work And No Play Makes Jack A Dull Boy
Section Self Promotion
Medium Digital
Brief The image was part of a pack of nine postcards, based around the theme of proverbs.

Circus
Section Editorial
Medium Digital
Brief The author went to a festival and saw Giffords Circus "a beacon of liberty and joy". He was eventually thrown out, for slashing an advertising banner as a protest against the rash of sponsors.
Commissioned by Nadia Rooney
Client The Ecologist

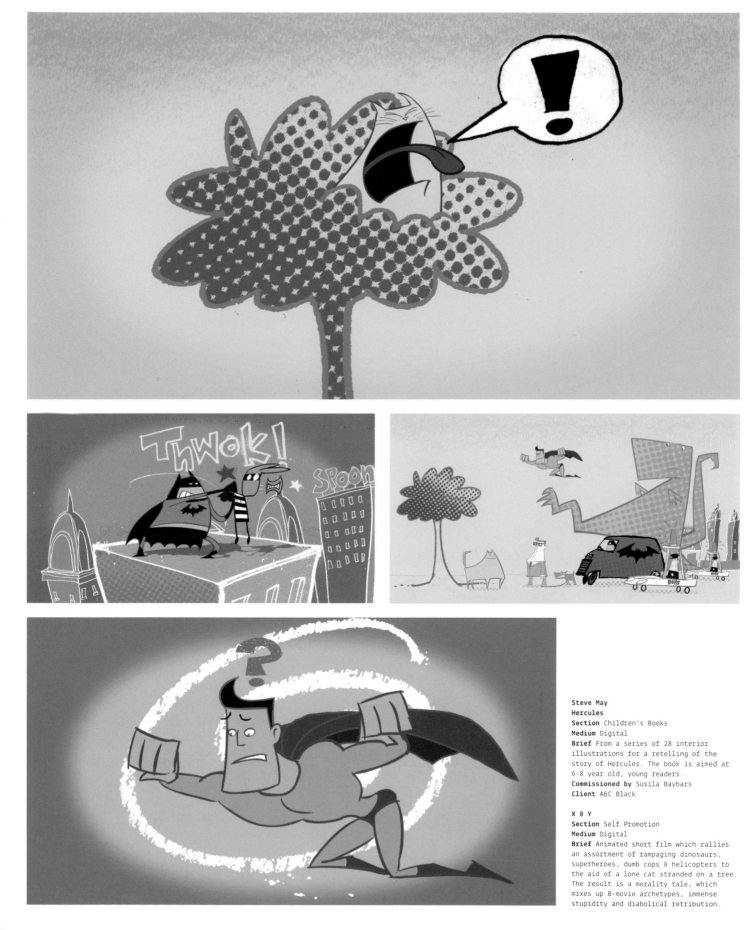

Steve May
Hercules
Section Children's Books
Medium Digital
Brief From a series of 28 interior
illustrations for a retelling of the
story of Hercules. The book is aimed at
6-8 year old, young readers.
Commissioned by Susila Baybars
Client A&C Black

X & Y
Section Self Promotion
Medium Digital
Brief Animated short film which rallies
an assortment of rampaging dinosaurs,
superheroes, dumb cops & helicopters to
the aid of a lone cat stranded on a tree.
The result is a morality tale, which
mixes up B-movie archetypes, immense
stupidity and diabolical retribution.

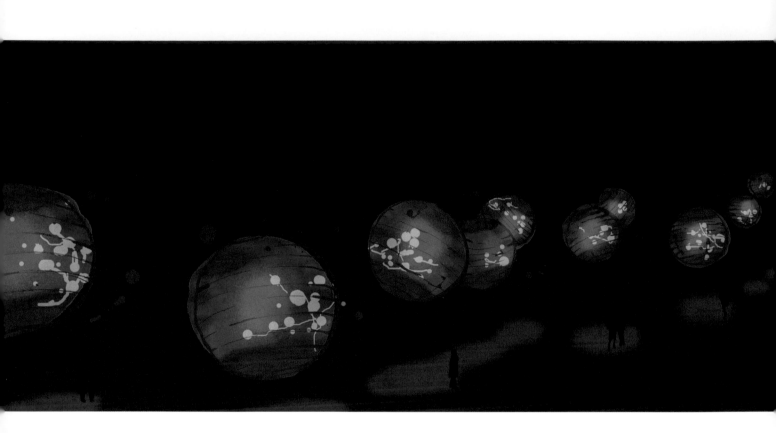

Lotte Oldfield /
The Festival Of Lights
Section Self Promotion
Medium Pen and ink, digital
Brief The Festival of Lights is a piece
of personal work taken from a series of
images inspired by dreams. Its purpose
was to convey ideas of spectacle, awe
and wonder and communicating the surreal
qualities of dream-imagery by playing
with perspective and scale.

>
Naomi Ryder /
Hayward Gallery
Section Design
Medium Thread on silk chiffon
Brief To be inspired by any events from
the Literature festival programme 2008 and
to exhibit at the Queen Elizabeth Hall,
Southbank, with the piece. My chosen event
and inspiration was a debate about The Hayward
gallery turning 40 and how artists respond
to their architecture during the festival.
The silk chiffon curtain I made was of 10
illustrated, embroidered gallery exteriors
with The Hayward gallery as the centrepiece.
Commissioned by Rachel Toogoode
Client Queen Elizabeth Hall at the Southbank
Commissioned for literary festival Aug 2008

Andy Smith /
Watch This Space
Section Self Promotion
Medium Silkscreen, digital
Brief Create an interesting, bold image
based around the slogan 'watch this
space' that integrates typography and
illustration. The final image will be
screenprinted as a poster.

Viewing Is Recommended...
Section Advertising
Medium Digital
Brief Illustrate the headline' Viewing
is recommended, especially at night'
with a couple viewing houses surrounded
by monsters.
Commissioned by Paul Belford
Client This Is Real Art
Commissioned for fish4.co.uk

Vic Turnbull /
Footprints
Section Self Promotion
Medium Scraperboard
Brief Self Promotion.

The Owl And The Pussycat
Section Self Promotion
Medium Scraperboard and digital media
Brief Self Promotion.

>

Mark Timmins /
The Good, The Bad & The Ugly
Section Editorial
Medium Collage and Photoshop
Brief To illustrate three different
scenarios in relation to future
investments in the economy.
Commissioned by
Maggie Williams and Bob Campion
Client Newsquest Specialist Media
Commissioned for
Engaged Investor Magazine

Tim Marrs /
SOL Summer
Section Advertising
Medium Digital and mixed media
Brief To capture the mood of summer,
Mexico and the fresh taste of SOL.
Commissioned by Grant Bryne
Client Leith Agency
Commissioned for SOL Beer

Grassed Up
Section Editorial
Medium Digital and mixed media
Brief Business price fixing, bribes and
informants...sounds like the Sweeney?
The office of Fair Trading are stamping
down, with payments to informants as much
as £100 000.
Commissioned by Gary Cook
Client Cook Design
Commissioned for Legal Business magazine

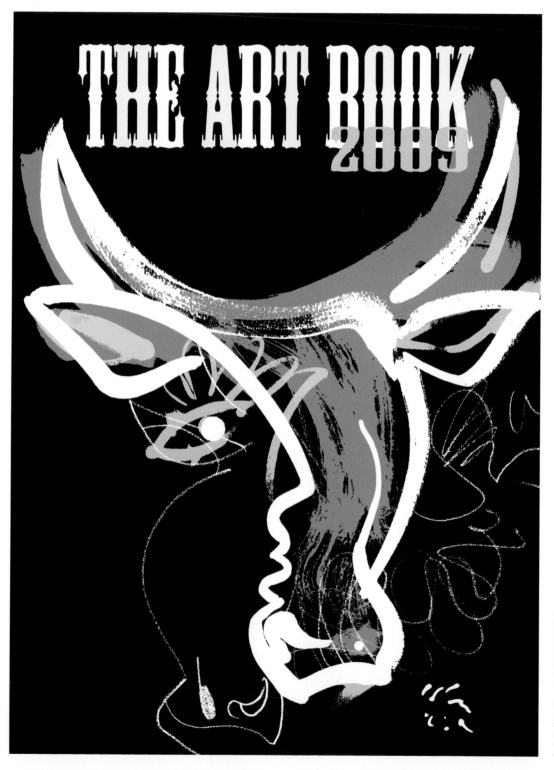

Brian Grimwood /
Grimwood 3
Section Design
Medium Brush, paint, computer, collage
Brief One of a series for Raffles
Hotel Singapore.
Commissioned by Robert Logan
Client Raffles Hotel

Grimwood 2
Section Books
Medium Brush, paint, computer, crayon
Brief Produce a front cover image.
Commissioned by John pigeon
Client The Art Book cover

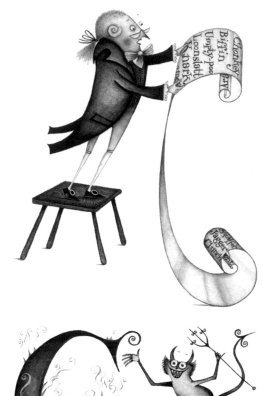

Clare Mackie
Section Books
Medium Watercolour and ink
A
Brief Abandannad - A stealer of handkerchiefs.
Late 18 - Mid 19 century.

Frontas Piece For Bingo Boys And Poodle Fakers
Brief To illustrate a person in period clothes
considering some of the words listed in the compendium
of historical slang.

G
Brief Gentleman in Black - The devil.
Mid 17 - 19 century.

Bingo Boys And Poodle Fakers Cover
Brief To illustrate the jacket for Bingo Boys and Poodle
Fakers, keeping the artwork in keeping with the period
when those terms were most used.
Commissioned by Joe Whitlock-Blundell
Client Folio Society

Green Man
Section Editorial
Medium Watercolour
Brief To illustrate a piece about the Green
Man for Country Life's My Week column.
Commissioned by Heather Lock
Client Country Life

In **1973**

there was a serious oil shortage.

U.S. imports of oil dropped from 1.2 million barrels

1.2m to barrels per day.

The price of oil quadrupled

$3 × 4 = $12

Schools and offices were forced to close to save on heating oil.

Closed   **CLOSED**

And factories cut production and laid off workers.

© Canadian Centre for Architecture 2007 © Maurizio Corraini srl 2007.

Aaargh I've run out of petrol. help!

Petrol pumps were empty.

Sorry

Not today, or tomorrow or the next day or the day after or the day after or...

SORRY NO PETROL

Sorry

I feel empty and unfulfilled

I feel so sad and empty I don't know what to do. This is awful, really.

I fondly remember the days when I used to serve customers daily. Now look at me! What use am I?

Oh, please stop going on so. You're not the only one who's suffering!

That was over **30** years ago but we are facing similar problems today.

Harriet Russell /
Sorry Out Of Gas
Section Books
Medium Mixed media
Brief To write and illustrate a short informative tale about oil crisis, alternative energies and housing that communicates to children in a fun and interesting way.
Commissioned by Giovanna Borasi
Client Canadian Centre for Architecture

>

Cheryl Taylor /
Be Free My Tweetheart
Section Self Promotion
Medium Photoshop, illustrator
Brief Self-initiated.

Alex Gardner /
Chilli Power
Section Editorial
Medium Digital
Brief To accompany an article about the
medical implications of the numbing
properties in chillis.
Commissioned by Jen Whiteley
Client Seven Publishing
Commissioned for Sainsbury's Magazine

Toby Leigh /
My Head Hurts
Section Self Promotion
Medium
Pen and ink, digital
Brief
Create an image bringing together
sketches, ideas and doodles from the
depths of my brain.

Tom Morgan-Jones
Section Children's Books
Medium Ink and digital
Commissioned by John Harris
Client notreallybooks
Brief Series of illustrations for "The Great
- The story of Beowulf and Grendel" by the
storyteller John Harris.

Looks Delicious
"Every night he'd lurch across the threshold
into the dark, decaying hall."

What to do?
"His Kingdom bought to its knees by a monster,
King Hrothgar feels helpless and worried."

Ouch
"They fastened the hook above the door frame
so that anyone who passed would see that they
had won their fight."

Would You Look At That
"Lifting his boot he discovered he'd stood on
an eye."

Nancy Tolford /
Key Girl
Section Self Promotion
Medium Digital
Brief
Self promotional piece adapted from
a published work about a woman who
organises parties with exclusive guest
lists in secretive locations.

Victoria Rose /
Captain Kittensworth /
Lady Kitty
Section Self Promotion
Medium Mixed media
Brief This is an amiable interpretation
of the well-loved characters from Jane
Austen's novel Pride & Prejudice. Captain
Kittensworth is based on Mr Darcy & Lady
Kitty on Elizabeth Bennet. My aim is to
create a story that children will enjoy,
adults will be able to relate to and
perhaps offer a refreshing take on times
gone by.

Katie Simpson /
Cockney
Section Self Promotion
Medium Digital
Brief Portrait of a cockney using
cockney rhyming slang.

Cat Leteve /
Cat And Mouse
Section Self Promotion
Medium Card, stitch and collage
Brief To illustrate a story by Kurt
Schwitters without making the strong
political and war-related
undertones obvious.

John Charlesworth / Evil Ink
Section Children's Books
Medium Digital
Brief A series of eight fiction books aimed at young,
disengaged teenage boys with a lower reading age.
Commissioned by Adrian Cole (Senior Editor, Franklin Watts)
Client Hachette Children's Books

Jamie Oliver /
Untitled
Section Self Promotion
Medium Mixed media
Brief An illustration for self-promotion.

Antony Cattini /
Survivor / **Descent** / **Fauna**
Section Self Promotion
Medium Watercolour, sand paper, Pantone
pen, Photoshop
Brief A series of landscape illustrations
portraying the incompatible relationships
between the inhabitants.

Stephen Wake /
The Stranger
Section Editorial
Medium Mixed media
Brief Illustrate an arresting image relating
to the title of the newspaper 'The Stranger'.
Commissioned by Aaron Huffman
Client The Stranger

Kevin Hauff
Poker Robot
Section Editorial
Medium Mixed and digital
Brief To create an illustration for a
Radio 4 documentary about a super robot
that will be designed to be unbeatable at
playing poker.
Commissioned by Hazel Brown
Client BBC Worldwide
Commissioned for Radio Times

Factory Relocation
Section Self Promotion
Medium Mixed and digital
Brief An experimental image exploring
the overseas relocation of many UK based
manufacturing businesses to reduce rising
labour costs.

Scorpion Bully
Section Self Promotion
Medium Mixed and digital
Brief An experimental image exploring how
office bullying and intimidation in the
work place is still going on, so causing
high stress levels for employees.

Gemma Latimer /
Teapot Man And Friends
Section Self Promotion
Medium Digital
Brief Characters from a series of
illustrations entitled the Tea Party. The
project explored the idiosyncratic and
eccentric qualities and elements of what
it is to be British.

Good Bad Conscience
Section Self Promotion
Medium Digital
Brief A lo-fi collage piece illustrating
good and bad conscience. The illustration
is about how we deal with our inner
demons and the choices we make, often
with a tendency to lean towards our
darker side.

Russell Walker /
2 HB
Section Self Promotion
Medium Mixed media
Brief Contribute to the
Central Illustration
Agency's online 'Print
Shop' and group exhibition.

<

Sim Marriott /
Dreamspark Installation
Section Advertising
Medium Digital
Brief 1 of 2 posters to attract
undergraduates to download free developer
tools from Dreamspark.
Commissioned by   Leanne Esposito
Client GT London
Commissioned for Dreamspark

Andrew Bylo /
Leading Figures In Advertising
Section Design
Medium Pencil
Brief To capture the essential character
of leading figures in advertising: Paul
Feldwick; Richard Storey: MC Saatchi; Dylan
Williams: Mother London; Jim Carroll: BBH.
Drawn from life.
Commissioned by Malcolm White
Client Krow Communications
Commissioned for The Account Planning Group

Tony Healey
Pope Benedict XVI
Section Editorial
Medium Ink and digital
Brief Supply caricature/ portrait of
Pope Benedict XVI for weekly Friday
profile piece.
Commissioned by Richard Oliver
Client The Telegraph Group

Philip Glenister
Section Editorial
Medium Ink and digital
Brief Supply caricature/ portrait of the
actor, Philip Glenister for weekly Friday
profile piece.
Commissioned by Wayne Caba
Client The Telegraph Group

Koichi Fujii /
The Great Voyage
Section Self Promotion
Medium Adobe Illustrator
and Photoshop
Brief The first
illustration for an
adventure story for
children about a journey
into the unknown and
the encounters faced.

Docteur William Fenouil

Madame Navet Maria

Jonathan Burton /
Saint Saen
Section Editorial
Medium 3D, collage, photography, Mac
Brief Composer of the Month section.
Illustrate Saint Saen concentrating on
his most popular and inventive work
entitled Carnival of the Animals.
Commissioned by Chris Barker
Client Haymarket Publishing
Commissioned for Classic FM Magazine

Docteur William Fenouil
Medium Fennel, collage,
Photography, Mac

Madame Navet Maria
Medium Turnip, dolls legs, collage,
photography, Mac

Madame Tintamarre
Medium Thyme, dolls legs, collage,
photography, Mac

Philippe Chouchou
Medium Cauliflower, doll legs and
arms, collage, photography, Mac

Section Self Promotion
Brief A personal project to play with
juxtaposing unusual found imagery,
which in this case was the content
of my fridge with a history of art
book. Produced in collaboration with
photographer Sophie Pawlak.

Madame Tintamarre

Philippe Chouchou

KARYL-JOZEF, HEAD ZOOKEEPER AT KLODENÁN ZOO, WAS ALWAYS LATE FEEDING THE WALRUS, KASZIA.

MASDA PYPEVSKA SELLS TICKETS TO THE ZOO. "3 KÓROUNY, PLEASE!"

HANDYMAN JIRZY HAILS FROM THE SCHLAVKA MOUNTAINS. HE WORKS HARD, EVEN AFTER MANY VODKA.

MADAME VLATSKA RUNS THE ZOO TEA-SHOP, KAFE DARWINA. SHE SERVES HOT SPICED CHAI & DEVILLED EGGS. SHE LOVES TITTLE-TATTLE.

OLD VAREK SITS ON THIS BENCH NEAR THE SNAKE-HOUSE EVERY DAY, CRACKING WALNUTS.

Paul Bommer /
Klodznán Zoo
Section Self Promotion
Medium Mixed media
Brief Various characters who work at
the Zoo in the city of Klodznán, capital
of a fictional Eastern European
country, Kasmirovja.

Mechanocchio
Section Books
Medium Mixed media
Brief A collaborative comic book
featuring a collection of different
artists, each contributing work based
on a theme. For volume 1 the theme
was Robot.
Commissioned by Jamie Smart
Client Fat Chunk
Commissioned for Fat Chunk: Vol 1:
Robot SLG Publishing

Life, The Universe And Kensington
Section Editorial
Medium Mixed media
Brief A Martian's Guide to the Proms.
Commissioned by Roger Browning
Client The Guardian

Becky Brown /
Dalmatian
Section Design
Medium Ink
Brief To create a series of engaging
and characterful animals for a range
of greetings cards to appeal to a wide
audience. This is one of several that
were chosen for publication.
Commissioned by Nicole Mendelsohn
Client The Almanac Gallery

Chris Haughton
Europe vs Microsoft
Section Editorial
Medium Digital
Brief Europe successfully sued Microsoft
for the largest sum in damages ever
awarded. The writer argued that moves
to restrict the business environment
such as this only succeed in frightening
businesses to move to the USA and Asia.
Commissioned by Steven Traylor
Client European Business Magazine

A Bit Lost
Section Children's Books
Medium Digital
Brief Front cover for a children's book
that I have written and illustrated.
Commissioned by Ines Yoo
Client BorimPress

Jungmin Son /
Go Back Home
Section Self Promotion
Medium Mixed media and digital
Brief Self promotion.

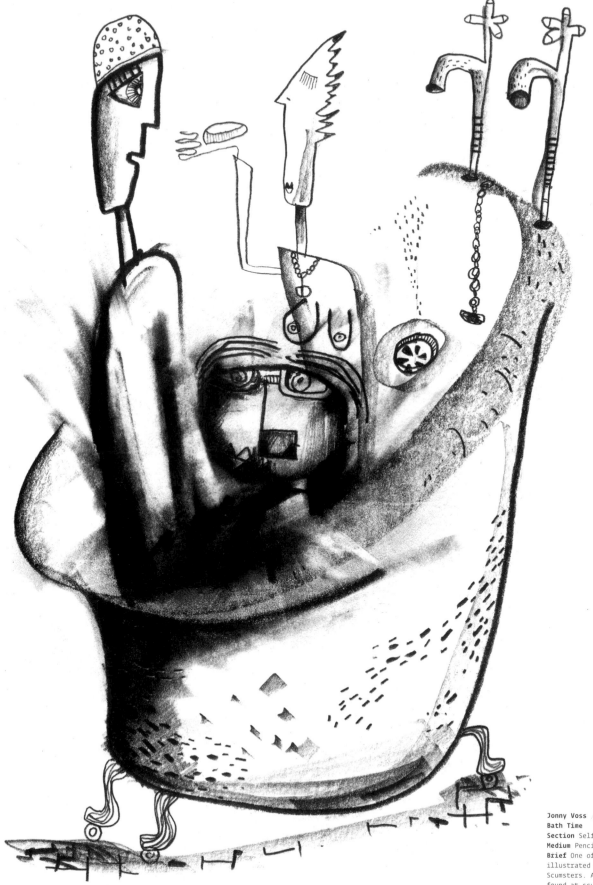

Jonny Voss
Bath Time
Section Self Promotion
Medium Pencil
Brief One of a number of drawings for the illustrated short story series titled Scumsters. A selection of these can be found at scumsters.co.uk.

Michelle Thompson /
Baby Steps
Section Editorial
Medium Digital
Brief Illustrate article on writing a
book gradually, day by day.
Commissioned by Kathy DeZarn
Client F & W Publications
Commissioned for Writers Digest magazine

Intercourse
Section Editorial
Medium Digital
Brief Book reviews of three sexually
related books.
Commissioned by David Woodside
Client The Globe & Mail

Jennifer Robinson
Confused
Section Self Promotion
Medium Acrylics
Brief Self promotion -
based around the idea of
a stressful enviroment.

Phil Wheeler /
Possibility Landscape
Section Advertising
Medium Digital
Brief Open brief to create web materials
for online promotion of a new beer for
urban design-oriented drinker. Based
around the slogan 'Everything
is possible'.
Commissioned by Jessica Bauer-Greene
Client Flavorpill
Commissioned for Budweiser

Lara Harwood /
Systems Thinking
Section Editorial
Medium Mixed media
Brief to illustrate an abstract concept of
"Systems Thinking" involving interacting with
and balancing out "bubbles". Please don't ask
me how it works!
Commissioned by Marie-Claire Camp
Client BBK Studio
Commissioned for Herman Miller / Jugglezine

The Boat Race
Section Advertising
Medium Mixed medium
Brief To create a design to
promote the Oxford and Cambridge
Boat Race for posters on the
London Underground.
Commissioned by Paul Crowley
Client Creator
Commissioned for
Transport For London

Engine Creative: Dan Smith /
Renaissance Anthems
Section Design
Medium Photoshop and Illustrator
Brief Striking collage artwork for
Renaissance club brand.
Commissioned by Tal Watson
Client Ministry of Sound

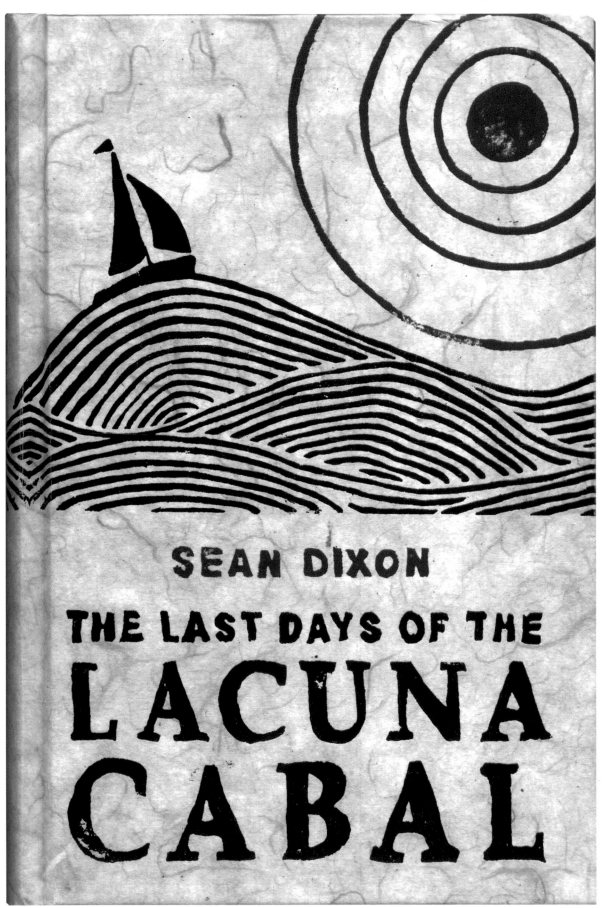

SEAN DIXON

THE LAST DAYS OF THE
LACUNA
CABAL

Becca Thorne /
The Last Days Of
The Lacuna Cabal
Section Self Promotion
Medium Linoprint on
handmade paper
Brief Winning entry in
competition to design
the front cover for Sean
Dixon's debut novel. Run
by Saatchi Online and
HarperCollins.

Frazer Hudson /
CCTV Loud-Hailer
Section Editorial
Medium Digital
Brief Create an illustration in response
to CCTV cameras now being fitted with
loud-hailers.
Commissioned by Gina Cross
Client The Guardian

Storm In A Tea Cup
Section Editorial
Medium Digital
Brief Create an illustration in response
to our fascination with 'rolling news'
items, which have the effect of turning
every minor event into a National crisis.
Commissioned by Gina Cross
Client The Guardian

Corporate specimens – the 'team player'

Chris Long
Be Yourself!
Section Editorial
Medium Acrylic
Brief To accompany an article by author
Melissa Bank on teenage identity crisis.
I wanted to create a carefree mood and a
sense of speed. I always love the fiery
red that trees can turn this season, so
she had to have auburn hair too.
Commissioned by Mike Reddy
Client Seventeen Magazine US

Pascale Carrington
Corporate Specimens
Section Self Promotion
Medium Ink, watercolour and digital
Brief Illustrate variety of personality
types found in the corporate world.

‹

Yoko Furusho /
Section Self Promotion
Medium Ink and acrylic
Brief A Japanese girl in nightgown.

Sandrine Dubois /
Safari
Section Design
Medium Digital, then vinyl print
Brief Create an environment on Safari theme for the new children care development at GOSH: 2 fresco with 6 animals in situation.
Client NHS Great Ormond Street Hosptial for children

Cathy Fisher
Finding The Monkey
Section Self Promotion
Medium Gouache pastel
and pencil crayon
Brief Image from a
series for a proposed
children's book.

Matthew Cook
Statue of Kim Il Sung, N Korea
Section Editorial
Medium Acrylic inks
Brief Travel to the Democratic
People's Republic of Korea
and draw and write about your
experiences during their
celebrations for the Korean War.
Commissioned by Hanya Yanagihara
Client Conde Nast NY
Commissioned for
October Issue Traveller

Florence Boyd /
Handmaids Tale
Section Books
Medium Relief print
Brief To illustrate an image for the book
jacket of novel 'The Handmaids Tale' by
Margaret Atwood.
Commissioned by Michael Salu
Client Random House

Thea Brine /
Doris Lessing
Section Editorial
Medium Mixed, digital
Brief Portray Doris Lessing.
Commissioned by Roger Browning
Client The Guardian
Commissioned for The Guardian Review Cover

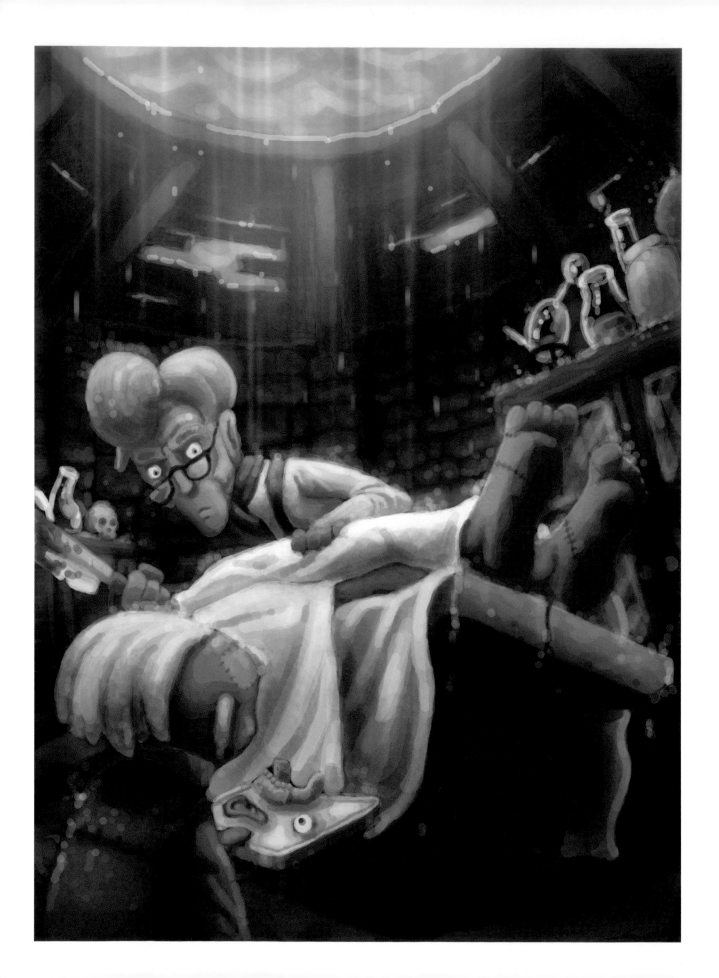

Ciaran Collins
Dr Frankenstein
Section Self Promotion
Medium Digital
Brief Simple child friendly, self-
promotional piece with a horror theme.
Light hearted and clichéd with an
emphasis on atmosphere.

Mark Frudd
The Good Life
Section Editorial
Medium Pencil and digital
Brief Illustration to support an article
about shopping locally and supporting
locally-sourced produce including growing
your own, improving the freshness of the
food on your plate and doing your bit for
the environment.
Commissioned by Richard Spencer
Client Kindred
Commissioned for
Benenden Healthcare Society

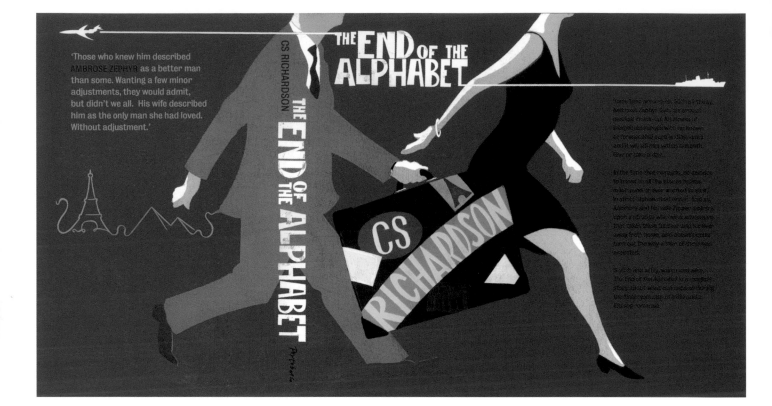

Andy Bridge /
The End Of The Alphabet
Section Books
Medium Emulsion on wood
Brief Evocative of adventure and
narrative and the exotic, also the life-
long romance between the main character
and his wife; the kind of object you feel
compelled to pick up and own/ which you
want to give as a present to your ideal
travelling companion.
Commissioned by Laura Barber
Client Portobello Books

Sophia Augusta Pankenier /
Plats Leipzig
Section Self Promotion
Medium Ink, paper and photography
Brief To illustrate the concept behind
the artist collective 'Plats' for
their exhibition in Leipzig. 'Plats'
is a collection of artists of various
mediums working collaboratively and
independently. 'Plats' is a creative
space, and a collective place.

Steven Carroll /
Fergus McCann
Section Books
Medium Scraperboard
Brief To illustrate the saviour of Celtic
Football Club Fergus McCann for 'The
Celtic Opus'.
Commissioned by Graeme Murdoch
Client Kraken Sport & Media Limited

\>
Joyce MacDonald /
The Pig In The Kitchen
Section Self Promotion
Medium Watercolour

Joyce Macdonald

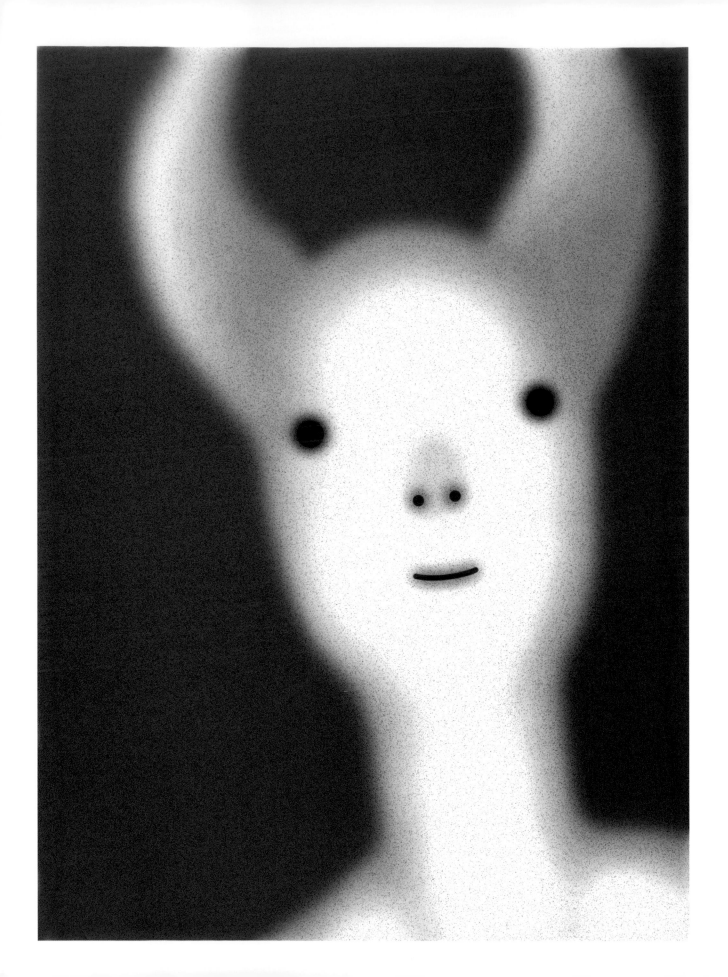

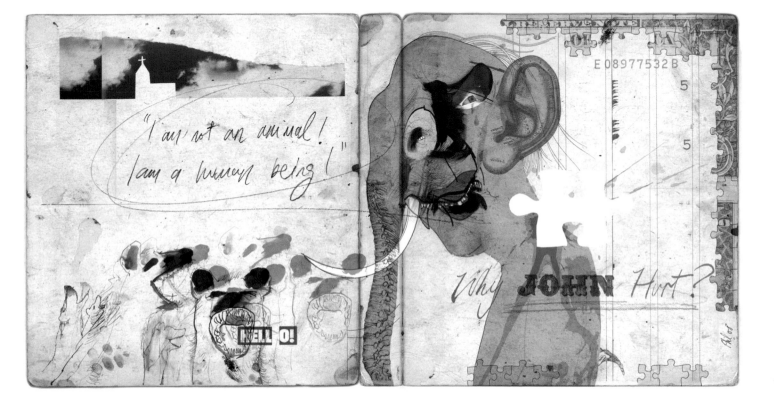

Stuart Briers /
I Dreamed Of Jophus
Section Self Promotion
Medium Digital
Brief A depiction of 'Jophus', a
character who repeatedly appears in the
dreams of a young boy. Part of a project
in development.

Philip Disley /
Why John Hurt?
Section Self Promotion
Medium Pen, ink, Photoshop
Brief To produce a cover for The Black
Book involving a missing jigsaw piece
mystery element.The shape,size and
position of missing piece were provided.

Dean Beattie /
The Night Train
Section Self Promotion
Medium Acrylics, pencils, Photoshop
Brief The presence of two shady youths
on the train makes the idea of public
transport even more unappealing
than usual.

Laura Clark /
Winter At The Royal Botanic Garden
Section Design
Medium Acrylic on paper
Brief Show that even in winter, the
Gardens are an enjoyable place to spend
time. An overly botanical depiction of
the plants is to be avoided.
Commissioned by Hamish Adamson
Client Royal Botanic Garden Edinburgh

<
Jo Davies /
Lighthouse
Section Design
Medium Gouache
Brief Thinking of you.
Commissioned by Nick Adsett
Client Nick Adsett Design

Allan Deas /
Bobbin Characters
Section New Media
Medium Pen and ink and digital
Brief To create a series of characters
to promote the full range of bicycles
for sale. Each character representing a
different style of bike.
Commissioned by Bobbin Bicycles
Client bobbinbicycles.co.uk

A. Richard Allen /
Match
Section Self Promotion
Medium Mixed media: pencil,
acrylic, digital
Brief A postcard image based on a
sketchbook piece - A crowd gaping at
a miniature man. I wanted to hint at a
narrative and also to explore a range
of expressions.

Dettmer Otto /
Bugged
Section Editorial
Medium Digital
Brief I bugged my husband's office and
caught him flirting with his secretary.
Commissioned by Richard Turley
Client The Guardian

21st Century Media
Section Editorial
Medium Digital
Brief Twenty-first century media. Coming
at you from all directions, all of the
time, in a variety of formats. Even the
people who run and distribute channels
don't really know what's going on.
Commissioned by Pat McNamee
Client Time Out

Russell Cobb

Find Your Pathway
Section Design
Medium Ink
Brief To produce a series of
illustrations for a creative skills and
development company's annual report.
The concept plays on idea of finding your
correct pathway.
Commissioned by Mark Benham
Client Shout Design
Commissioned for ArtsMatrix

**The Illustrators Guide To Law And
Business Practice**
Section Books
Medium Mixed media
Brief To illustrate an inventive and eye
catching wrap around Cover for the AOI's
law and business guide. A visual play
on the idea of understanding and over
coming the obstacles that may arise in
the industry.
Commissioned by Derek Brazell
Client Association of Illustrators

Time For Decay
Section Self Promotion
Medium Mixed media
Brief One of a series of self initiated images produced on the theme of nature. The image focuses on the nature decaying in autumn time.

Memories Of Nature
Section Self Promotion
Medium Mixed media
Brief One of a series of self initiated images produced on the theme of nature. The image focuses on collected observations and memories.

Full Bloom
Section Self Promotion
Medium Mixed media
Brief One of a series of self initiated images produced on the theme of nature. the image focuses on nature blooming into colour.

The German Philosopher
Section Self Promotion
Medium Mixed media
Brief One of a series of images produced for an exhibition creating characters inspired by found images and books.

fig 68.

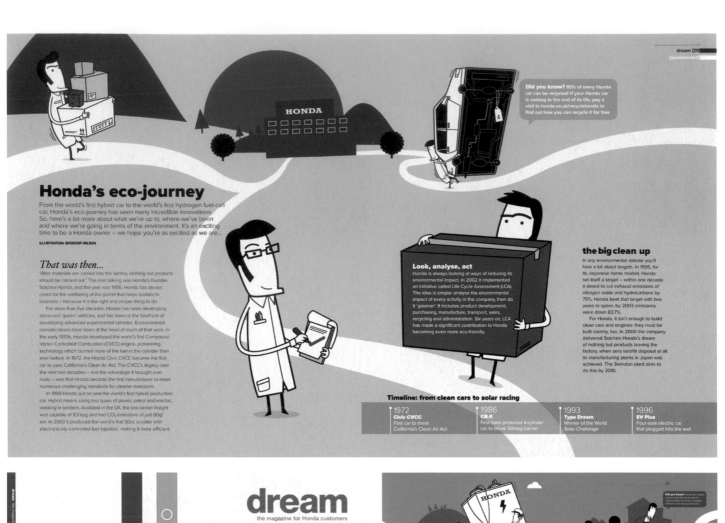

Honda's eco-journey

From the world's first hybrid car to the world's first hydrogen fuel-cell car, Honda's eco-journey has seen many incredible innovations. So, here's a bit more about what we're up to, where we've been and where we're going in terms of the environment. It's an exciting time to be a Honda owner – we hope you're as excited as we are...

ILLUSTRATION: SPENCER WILSON

That was then...

"After materials are carried into the factory, nothing but products should be carried out." The man talking was Honda's founder, Soichiro Honda, and the year was 1956. Honda has always cared for the wellbeing of the planet that helps sustain its business – because it is the right and proper thing to do.

For more than five decades, Honda has been developing advanced 'green' vehicles, and has been at the forefront of developing advanced experimental vehicles. Environmental considerations have been at the heart of much of that work. In the early 1970s, Honda developed the world's first Compound Vortex Controlled Combustion (CVCC) engine, pioneering technology which burned more of the fuel in the cylinder than ever before. In 1972, the Honda Civic CVCC became the first car to pass California's Clean Air Act. The CVCC's legacy over the next two decades – and the advantage it brought over rivals – was that Honda became the first manufacturer to meet numerous challenging standards for cleaner emissions.

In 1999 Honda put on sale the world's first hybrid production car. Hybrid means using two types of power, petrol and electric, working in tandem. Available in the UK, the two-seater Insight was capable of 83mpg and had CO_2 emissions of just 80g/km. In 2003 it produced the world's first 50cc scooter with electronically-controlled fuel injection, making it more efficient.

Did you know? 85% of every Honda car can be recycled! If your Honda car is coming to the end of its life, pay a visit to honda.co.uk/recyclehonda to find out how you can recycle it for free

Look, analyse, act

Honda is always looking at ways of reducing its environmental impact. In 2002 it implemented an initiative called Life Cycle Assessment (LCA). The idea is simple: analyse the environmental impact of every activity in the company, then do it 'greener'. It includes product development, purchasing, manufacture, transport, sales, recycling and administration. Six years on, LCA has made a significant contribution to Honda becoming even more eco-friendly.

the big clean up

In any environmental debate you'll hear a lot about targets. In 1995, for its Japanese home market, Honda set itself a target – within one decade it aimed to cut exhaust emissions of nitrogen oxide and hydrocarbons by 75%. Honda beat that target with two years to spare; by 2003 emissions were down 83.7%.

For Honda, it isn't enough to build clean cars and engines: they must be built cleanly, too. In 2000 the company delivered Soichiro Honda's dream of nothing but products leaving the factory, when zero landfill disposal at all its manufacturing plants in Japan was achieved. The Swindon plant aims to do this by 2010.

Timeline: from clean cars to solar racing

1972	1986	1993	1996
Civic CVCC First car to meet California's Clean Air Act	**CR-X** First mass produced 4-cylinder car to break 50mpg barrier	**Type Dream** Winner of the World Solar Challenge	**EV Plus** Four-seat electric car that plugged into the wall

dream
the magazine for Honda customers

discover the world's cleanest car
meet three modern multi-taskers
drive the 2008 Honda S2000
win a designer eco-accessory

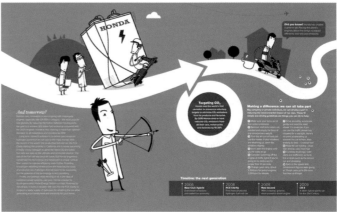

And tomorrow?

Timeline: the next generation

2006	2008	2008	2009

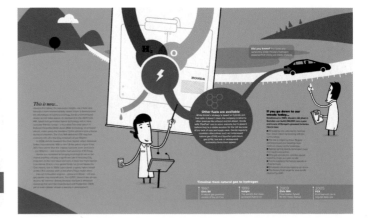

This is now...

Other fuels are available

If you go down to our woods today...

Timeline: from natural gas to hydrogen

1997	1999	2001	2005

*In one year,
a car can produce
4 times
its own weight in carbon dioxide.

be good, drive small

* http://www.wycombe.gov.uk/sitePages.asp?step=4&contentID=623&categoryID=321

*People in England
and Wales
consume about
150 litres
of water every day

be good, use water wisely

* http://www.environment-agency.gov.uk/yourenv/eff/1190084/people_lifestyles/household/?version=1&lang=_e

*Glass produced from
recycled glass instead
of raw materials
reduces
related air pollution by 20%,
and water pollution by 50%

be good, recycle

* http://library.thinkquest.org/11353/facts.htm

*By
turning down
your central heating thermostat
one degree,
fuel consumption is cut by as much as **10%**

be good, turn it down a bit

Spencer Wilson /
Honda Dream (Cover) /
Honda Dream (Past) /
Honda Dream (Present) /
Honda Dream (Future) /
Section Editorial
Medium Digital
Brief Illustrate the
continuing green
credentials of Honda
and their cars from the
past to the present and
looking forward into
the future.
Commissioned by
Philip Terrett
Client
River Publishing Ltd
Commissioned for
Honda Dream magazine

Be Good...
Section Self Promotion
Medium Digital
Brief Using internet
facts about resource
usage to create a
series of images to
promote a new direction
in my work.

Olivier Kugler /
King's Arms
Section Editorial
Medium Mixed media
Brief Create a drawing for a spread about
life in London. The Art Director told me
I can do whatever I want...
Commissioned by Quintin Leeds
Client XXI - Vingtetun

<
Adrian Valencia /
Girls, Flowers And Rain
Section Self Promotion
Medium Digital
Brief Self generated.

Lesley Barnes /
The Lady Of Shalott 'The Mirror Cracked' /
The Lady Of Shalott 'I Am Half Sick Of Shadows' /
The Lady of Shalott 'Weave The Mirrors Magic Sights' /
Section Self Promotion
Medium Papercuts and digital
Brief Concept drawings for an animated representation
of the poem 'The Lady of Shalott'.

<

Satoshi Kambayashi /
High Achiever
Section Editorial
Medium Digital
Brief Ed Balls' suggestion that there is
no link between poverty and educational
attainment is an utter fantasy.
Commissioned by David Gibbons
Client New Statesman

China Story
Section Editorial
Medium Digital
Brief A country girl meets a Beijing boy.
An illustration for a short story.
Commissioned by David Gibbons
Client New Statesman

Paquebot /
Greetings From Brighton
Section Self Promotion
Medium Digital
Brief Create a humorous postcard
for Brighton.

NO DESIGN NO PARTY

Protagonisti: i vip e gli arredi, alla pari. Gli uni che alimentano gli altri e viceversa. La festa come cornice. Tra mondanità e progetto, il reportage del Salone
Illustrazioni Sarah Gooch
Testo di Roberta Mutti

Sarah Gooch /
Salone Del Mobile
Section Editorial
Medium
Line drawing, painting,
collage, digital
Brief To illustrate an
article about events
at Milan's furniture
fair, Salone del Mobile
2008. Including Cassina,
Lexus, Established &
Sons, Swarovski,
T Magazine and Versace.
Commissioned by
Chiara Rostoni
Client Case da Abitare

McFaul Studio /
Liverpool John Lennon Airport
Section Design
Medium Digital
Brief As Liverpool is European City of
Culture 2008 it was felt the Airport
needed a face lift before the masses
descended for its festivities. We
were approached to create over 350m of
continuous vinyl graphic, 20 column wraps
in baggage reclaim and 7 airside bus
wraps not to mention animation on the
main signage and buses.
Commissioned by Beverley Wood
Client Broome Jenkins
Commissioned for Liverpool John Lennon
Airport Portal project

Sound & Vision
Section Design
Medium Digital
Brief To give Sound & Vision (a Cancer
Research flagship event) a sophisticated
new 'look n' feel'.
Commissioned by Rob O'Conner
Client Stylo Rouge
Commissioned for Cancer Research

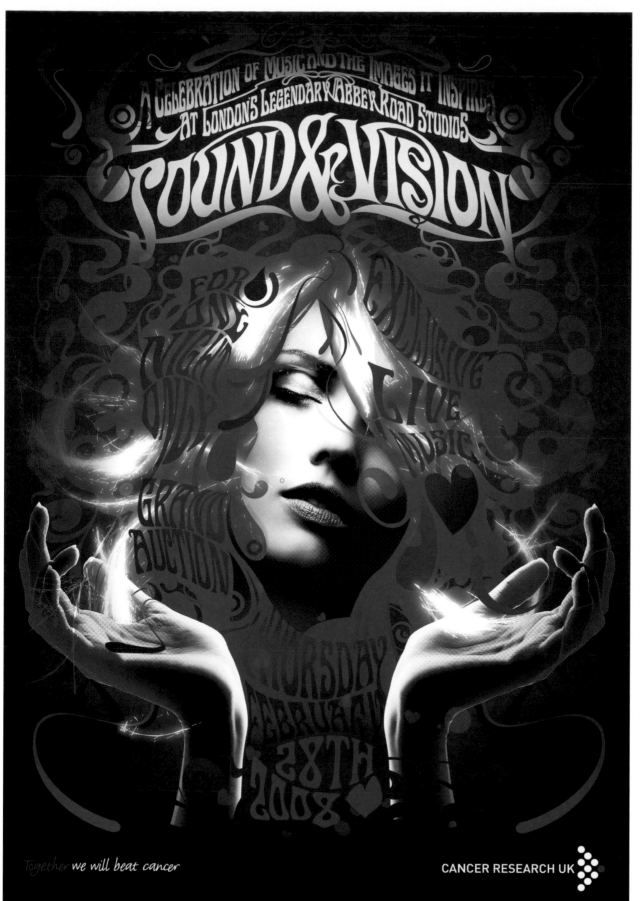

Jessie Ford
Blue Birds
Section Design
Medium Paper, paint and Mac
Brief To create a caring scene showing a
Mother and Father relationship with
their child.
Commissioned by Michelle Markee
Client Momentum Worldwide
Commissioned for Reclast/Novartis
Pharmaceuticals

Ballet Class
Section Self Promotion
Medium Paper, paint and Mac
Brief This is one spread from my most
recent children's book, showing the main
character running to her dance class.

Jonny Mendelsson /
Eerie Silence At Sea
Section Design
Medium Digital collage
Brief To produce an image for The Marine
Conservation Society's annual report. Overfishing
has meant a lack of food for seabirds, and plastic
waste has caused fatalties.
Commissioned by Marianne Steele
Client Marine Conservation Society

Sarah Hanson / **On The Road**
Section Books
Medium Collage
Brief Produce a cover illustration for
Jack Kerouac's book "On The Road" to
represent the journey of Sal and friend
Dean as they travel across America.
Commissioned by Sirida Pensri
Client Penguin

ELTON · JOHN
Red Piano Tour 2008

Paul Garland /
Coke Bottle
Section Self Promotion
Medium Mixed media
Brief To produce an image for the new
Coca Cola Zero product, enhancing the
zero sugars, fats and saturates.

Elton John
Section Self Promotion
Medium Mixed media
Brief Poster for Elton John 2008 tour.

Prick
Section Self Promotion
Medium Mixed media
Brief Response to 'Artful Todger' project
to be hung in an exhibition and printed
in a book, all proceeds to a Testicular
Cancer charity.

John Wayne
Section Self Promotion
Medium Mixed media
Brief Portrait of John Wayne to
include and highlight the details of
a recent biography.

Gail Armstrong
Section Children's Books
Medium Paper sculpture
Icarus And Daedalus Take Flight
Brief The Greek myth of Icarus and his father, Daedalus, tells of their escape from prison using wings they have made from fallen feathers and candle wax.

Feathers
Brief To create a front cover image to relate to the two very different stories in the book, but both with a theme of feathers and flight.

Icarus Falling
Brief Despite his father's warnings, Icarus flies higher and higher until the heat of the sun melts the wax in his wings and he falls as the wings disintegrate.
Commissioned by Stephanie Rice
Client Hampton-Brown/National Geographic
Commissioned for National Geographic Educational books

Andrew Pavitt /
The Hand That Feeds
Section Self Promotion
Medium Digital
Brief A self directed piece
reflecting the dilemma faced by the
Buddhist community in Burma.

Neal Fox /
Digested Read: Norman Mailer's
"The Castle In The Forest"
Section Editorial
Medium Mixed media

Brief Illustration for the Digested
Read: a weekly spot in G2 which casts an
sardonic view on recent releases. It is
the story of Adolf Hitler's childhood
as seen through the eyes of Dieter, a
demon sent to put him on his destructive
path. The novel explores the idea that
Hitler had no Jewish heritage but was the
product of incest.
Commissioned by Richard Turley
Client The Guardian G2 section

Digested Read:
Ian McEwan's "On Chesil Beach"
Section Editorial
Medium Mixed media
Brief The Digested Read is a weekly
column by John Crace which casts an eye
over recent releases. On Chesil Beach
focuses on a young newly wed couple
on their honeymoon, who are sexually
inexperienced.
Commissioned by Richard Turley
Client The Guardian G2 section

Sam Kerr /
If Boris Johnson Wins...
Section Editorial
Medium Mixed media
Brief If Boris Johnson wins next week....
it might be time to leave England and
move north, argues Ian Jack: Illustration
to depict writer, Ian Jack, flying the
Scottish flag in reaction to the London
Mayor's election. The illustration needed
to work with the text and be a dominant
feature on the page.
Commissioned by Izabella Bielawska
Client The Guardian

Annabel Wright /
**He Never Meant To Abandon His Son - He
Thought He Was Setting Him Free**
Section Editorial
Medium Mixed media
Brief The writer explains that did not
intend to abandon his child after the
breakdown of his marriage.
Commissioned by Sarah Habershon
Client The Guardian

Paddy Molloy /
**Don't Scratch Daley Out Of Britain's
Golden History**
Section Editorial
Medium Mixed media
Brief Illustrate Simon Hattenstone's
column about great Olympians, with a
deadline of five hours.
Commissioned by Gina Cross
Client The Guardian

Georgina Hounsome /
Is A Big Family Better Than A Small One?
Section Editorial
Medium Mixed media
Brief Illustrate readers' letters on
whether it's better to be a member of a
small or large family.
Commissioned by Sarah Habershon
Client The Guardian

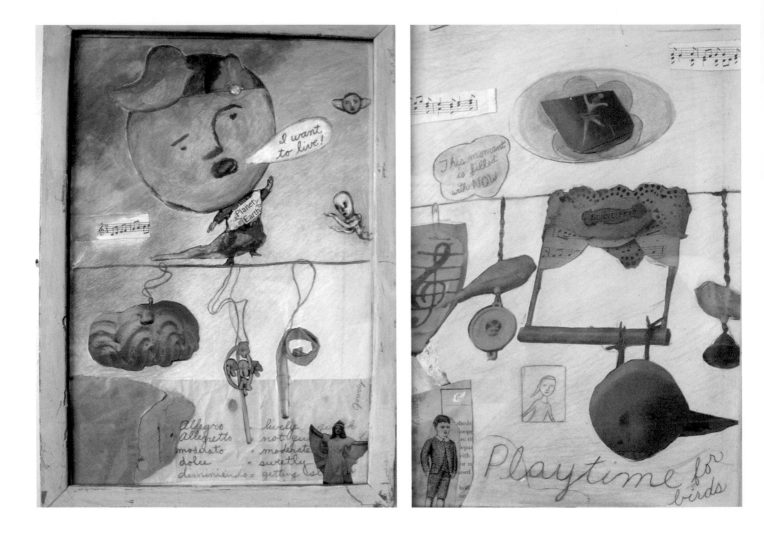

Carolyn Gowdy /
Life is an Adventure:
Life On The Wire /
Playtime For Birds /
Have A Nice Day /
Citizen Of The Planet
Section Self Promotion
Medium Mixed media
Brief Life is a gift.

Matt Murphy /
Body Bag Bombers
Section Self Promotion
Medium Collage
Brief Self promotional piece created
after watching the Americans bomb the
hell out of Iraq all night on BBC news
24! I wanted something to highlight the
fact that we seem to have distanced
ourselves emotionally from what
happens in war.

Oil
Section Self Promotion
Medium Collage
Brief Image created after hearing an
article on Radio 4 in May 2007 about the
possible rise of Russia in the global
economy thanks to it's control over oil
and other fuels.

Tom Hughes /
What Happened Next? At The Country Fair
Section Design
Medium Adobe Illustrator
Brief Illustrate "Before and After"
scenes for a 1000 piece Jigsaw.
Commissioned by Su Jones
Client Tiger Print - A division of
Hallmark Cards PLC

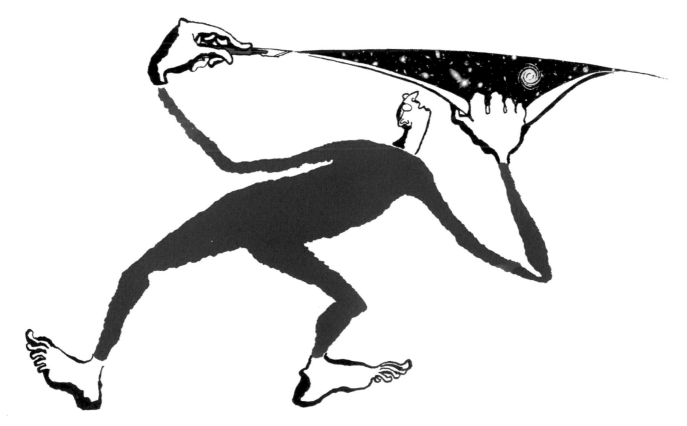

Belle Mellor
Post Detective
Section Editorial
Medium Pen and ink, collage, digital
Brief A new tracking device, small enough
to be slipped into an envelope, can
pinpoint hold-ups within postal services.
Commissioned by Una Corrigan
Client The Economist

Scratching The Surface Of The Universe
Section Editorial
Medium Pen and ink, collage, digital
Brief Huge steps are being taken into
the unknown reaches of particle physics
at the moment- however they will only
scratch the surface of the universe.
Commissioned by Una Corrigan
Client The Economist

Printing
Section Editorial
Medium Pen and ink, digital
Brief For an article on the benefits of
carrying out all stages of the printing
process in house.
Commissioned by Dinah Lone
Client Print Week

Peter Mac /
An Ordinary Worker In An Extraordinary World
Section Editorial
Medium
Adobe Illustrator, Photoshop and pencil
Brief Illustrate the lead article about the
red tape a drug/social worker has to go
through before they can help the client.
Commissioned by Max Daly
Client Druglink

Swim The Channel
Section Books
Medium
Adobe Illustrator, Photoshop and pencil
Brief For the book "Sod that, 103 things not
to do before you die". Depict the ineptitude
of swimming the channel.
Commissioned by Helen Ewing
Client The Orion Publishing Group Limited

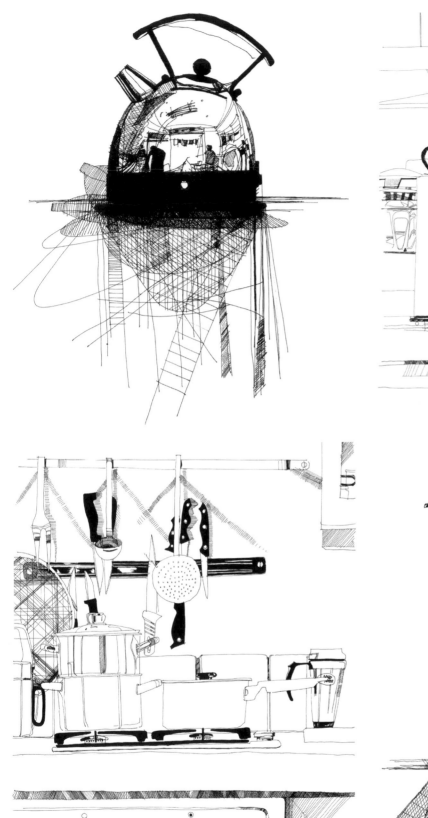

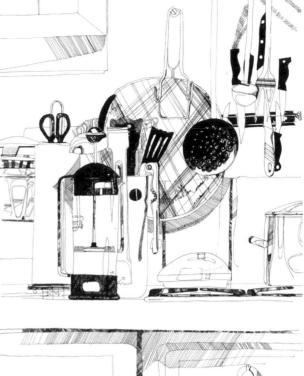

**Peter Hutchinson
Kitchen Series
Section** Self Promotion
Medium Pen and ink
Brief To capture the
spirit of vessels and
implements in every
day use in a kitchen
setting.

Justine Beckett
Involvement
Welcoming
Dynamics
People
Section Design
Medium Pen and Photoshop
Brief The brief was to create a set of illustrations that
expressed the ethos of ISOS Housing Limited, whose primary
role is to create thriving communities by providing
quality, affordable homes for people who need them.
This illustration needed to show their belief in working
together and the vital role that their staff play.
Commissioned by Gardiner Richardson
Client ISOS Housing Limited

Anne Chan Wai Ming /
The Beautiful Eyes Of Muse
Section Self Promotion
Medium Photoshop
Brief Dream on, even if only for one
day.... Muse (the main character of the
series) fills her world with fantasy,
passion, love and imagination, and brings
out "the little girl" who is hidden
inside of every woman. Happiness to her
is as simple as just like a butterfly
sitting on her shoulder some day, and
life to her, what it is but a dream.

Jonathan Gibbs
The Oak Tree
Section Advertising
Medium Wood engraving
Brief To represent an oak tree for the
promotion of recycling paper. Recycled
Christmas cards were attached to the
posters, gradually each day, to cover the
tree, between Christmas 2007 and the New
Year in Princes Street, Edinburgh.
Commissioned by Adrian Jeffery,
Brian McGregor & Tamsin Ansdell
Client Mightysmall
Commissioned for Woodland Trust Scotland

Crow Country
Section Books
Medium Wood engraving
Brief To illustrate a flight of rooks,
crows and jackdaws.
Commissioned by Anna Crone
Client Random House

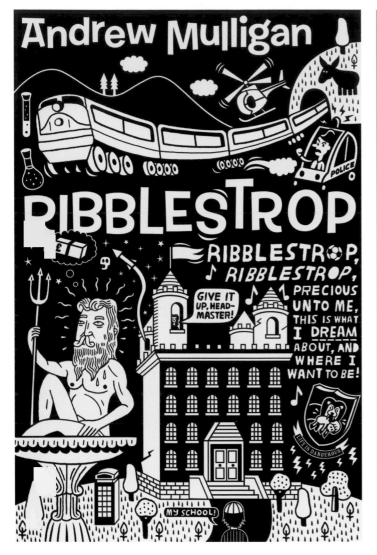

Serge Seidlitz /
Ribblestrop
Section Books
Medium Digital
Brief To illustrate the cover of the book
'Ribblestrop', with images from the novel.
Client Simon and Shuster

Los Angeles Times Football Cover
Section Editorial
Medium Digital
Brief To illustrate the route to the final
by two American colleges competing in the
college football league.
Commissioned by Derek Simmons
Client LA Times
Commissioned for Los Angeles Times

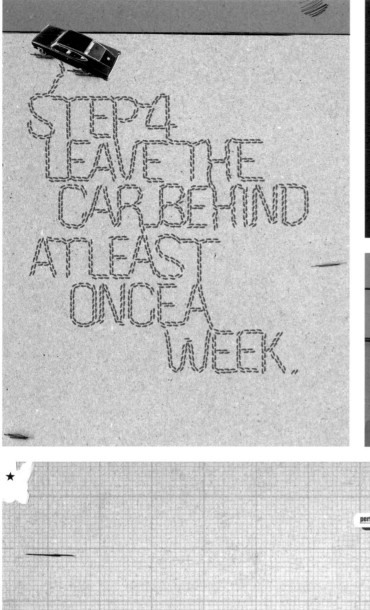

Caroline Tomlinson /
A Greener Scotland
Section Advertising
Medium Collage
Brief Scotland's national newspaper publish a
'green issue to inform the Scottish public about
'Ten Easy Steps' to a greener lifestyle,' Each
step illustrated how a simple change to daily
living can help the environment.
Commissioned by Kirsty Wright
Client Newhaven Advertising Agency
Commissioned for The Scottish Government

Business Targets
Section Editorial
Medium Collage
Brief To illustrate an article about the rising
targets in business today.
Commissioned by Erroll Jones
Client Caspian Publishing
Commissioned for Real Business Magazine

Jill Calder /
Spotted
Section Self Promotion
Medium Ink, paint and digital
Brief Create a child-friendly
image for my portfolio and to
sell as editioned prints.

The Selfish Giant's Garden
Section Self Promotion
Medium Ink
Brief Create a colourful poster
image for Oscar Wilde's "The
Selfish Giant's Garden" which
was being adapted for the
Chicago Children's Theatre.

Burufu
Section Books
Medium Ink and digital
Brief To illustrate Burufu,
a story about an evil magician
in The Caseroom Press's new
edition of "Utopian Tales from
Weimar" edited and translated
by Professor Jack Zipes.
The book features stories
by political activists who
deliberately transformed
traditional German fairy tales
into utopian narratives and
social commentary.
Commissioned by
Barrie Tullett
Client The Caseroom Press

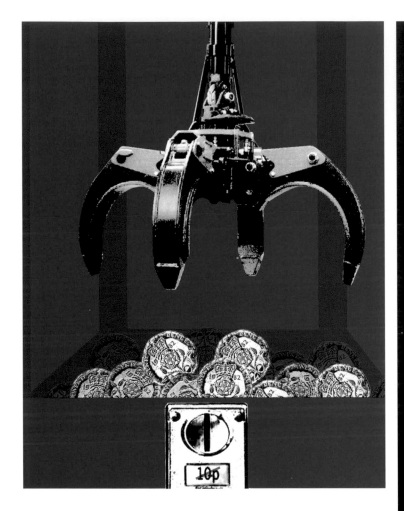

Tobias Hickey
Tax
Section Editorial
Medium Mixed media
Brief The negative impact of Labour's
abolition of the 10p tax band.
Commissioned by Gina Cross
Client The Guardian Newspaper
Commissioned for
The Guardian Comment page

Portrait of a City-New York
Section Editorial
Medium Mixed media
Brief Portrait of a city.
Commissioned by Katherine Masters
Client Highlife Magazine

While others sleep all together, huddled close at night.

Il Sung Na
ZZzzz
A Book of Sleep

Il Sung Na /
Zzzzz: A Book of Sleep
Section Children's Books
Medium Digital and mixed medium
Brief Create an original text and complimentary illustration for a 24-page picture book for the 0-5 age group.
Commissioned by Sarah Wilson
Client Meadowside Children's Books

Emily Bolam /
First Birthday / Ski Bunny
Section Self Promotion
Medium Acrylic
Brief Greetings card sample.

Hannah McVicar /
Planting by Numbers
Section Editorial
Medium Mixed medium
Brief To produce a floral border
illustration that inspires readers to
grow plants from seeds.
Commissioned by Grace Bradberry
Client The Times
Commissioned for The Saturday Times
Magazine, Gardening section

Beach /
David 1 Goliath 0
Section Books
Medium Digital
Brief Illustrate an imaginary football
duel in a playful and oblique way.
Commissioned by Jerzovskaja
Client Herzglut Verlag
Commissioned for Football Heroes See Red

Er Kommt / Er Kommt Nicht
Section New Media
Medium Digital
Brief Create a rogues gallery of
footballers past and present to welcome
the European Championship
to Switzerland.
Commissioned by Remo Prinz
Client Zattoo
Commissioned for Zattoo

Blasts From The Past
Section Editorial
Medium Digital
Brief Illustrate a Christmas Ghost
Story where academics begin to receive
posthumous help from the spirits of
former professors.
Commissioned by Alex Morgan
Client TSL Education
Commissioned for
Times Higher Education Supplement

Medical Mugging
Section Editorial
Medium Digital
Brief To accompany an article on the
shortage of geriatric doctors in the US.
Commissioned by Chris Barber
Client TSL Education
Commissioned for
Times Higher Education Supplement

i33 / New Talent

Works by full-time students, including those
graduated in 2008.

i33 / New Talent / Essay
Andrew Selby / Illustrator, Educator and Author

Andrew Selby is an award-winning illustrator who works extensively for publishing and advertising clients both nationally and internationally. His work has appeared in newspapers, on billboards and on the covers of major corporate reports for household names for nearly two decades.

He is Programme Coordinator for the Visual Communication programmes at Loughborough University. His research interests contextualise the subject of illustration and question its perceived 'place' in the expanding context of visual communication, unearthing areas for further examination that stem from the interdisciplinary and cross-disciplinary nature of the subject, through books, articles and journal papers. He is the author of Animation in Process (2009), published by Laurence King.

In early 2009, I travelled to Seattle to give a paper entitled, 'The Adventures of Gary Baseman: Dumb Luck or Brilliant Creative Strategy?' at the Interdisciplinary Design Institute at Washington State University. For me, Californian illustrator, designer, producer and director Baseman represents a number of qualities one needs to be perennially successful in the field: bright, articulate, absorbing, arresting, confident and charming. These attributes go beyond the codes and conditions of creation, and instead speak to a much wider plane of sensibilities, namely those of marketing, business acumen, enterprise, affinity with technology and an interest in micro-trends.

In the audience for the paper were a range of American graduate students from the fields of architecture, product and industrial design, brought up on a diet of nineties grunge, littered with a mix of visual culture and hybridised into the melting pot of Pop Surrealism. Through the disjointed and arguably discredited American political and social landscape of the last decade, these graduate students bristled with the excitement of knowing that promised change was now within touching distance, with the inauguration of then President-elect Obama only 48 hours away. The energy and the optimism in that lecture hall sat in complete contrast to the rain-soaked Heathrow airport that I had left, with giant screens in Terminal 5 streaming a constant torrent of credit crunch woes.

In Seattle, I never heard the term 'credit crunch' once. Indeed, I used the rest of my visit to talk to independent artists and creators, across a broad platform of the visual arts, about the state of the nation in the context of creative directions. The result was an overriding feeling of opportunity through change: that old initiatives had been publicly declared moribund and new expectations had already begun to take seed and break the surface, no doubt incubated by the impending arrival of the most eagerly awaited leader since John F. Kennedy. He was in danger of being engulfed before even being sworn in.

I believe new talents require space to grow and that inevitably means taking a chance with some unknown varieties. I'm going to argue that some attributes should be a given, rather than a risk. These new illustrators can make compelling images; they have an ability to communicate ideas, thoughts and feelings; they can work to deadlines. These fundamentals need exercising through the creative fusion that exists between a challenging brief and thoughtful art direction. Then we can concentrate not on the decoration but on the content - substance over style. That's the future of intelligent illustration. It listens then it speaks.

In times of adversity, new talents need to be progressive, by displaying an ability to forge opportunities, research untapped target markets, employ their communication skills in ever-wider contexts and publicise and promote these successes in effective and thoughtful ways. If being a creator is a given – being the audience for what has been produced is equally vital - but frequently overlooked. The audience is intelligent. Yes, it wants style, but it craves content. It's not dumb luck – it's a brilliant creative strategy.

Amy graduated from the University of
Plymouth in 2008 with a BA in Illustration.
During her time there she had a chance
to experiment and develop her style and
way of working. Amy likes to produce her
work by hand, using lots of different
media, including sewing, lino and relief
printing, collage, drawing and stenciling.
Her inspirations and ideas come from myths,
superstitions, dream psychology, stories
and folklore. She is interested in making
and illustrating her own books based around
these subjects. She is currently living and
working in Oxford.

This image came from a project based
around ideas of superstition, folklore and
Victorian dream analysis. A selection of the
final images were then made into a book.

College University of Plymouth
Medium Collage
Brief One of a series of images based upon the reading
of dreams. This dream is about imminent engagement.
Course Leader Ashley Potter
Course BA Illustration

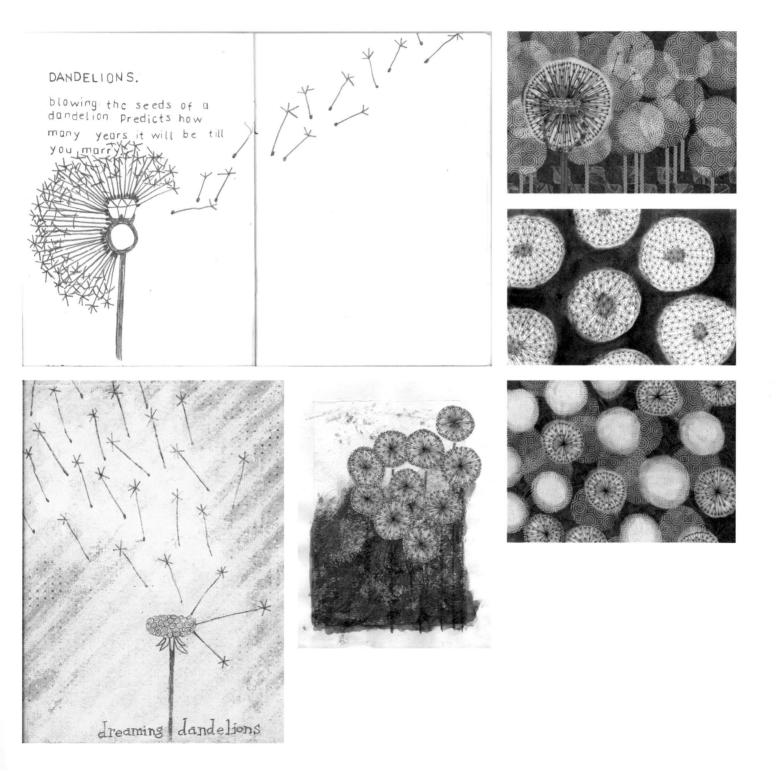

i33 / New Talent Refresh! Award / Silver

Sponsored by The Coningsby Gallery /
Lizzie Mary Cullen / Psychogeography

Lizzie Mary Cullen specialises in situationist illustration, mapping municipal areas to create a tactile, sensual and captivating journey. She is being published for several projects during 2009, and is exhibiting with the Cynthia Corbett Gallery early next year. Currently she lives and works in London, and spends time in New York, psychogeographically mapping the city.

College Goldsmiths College
Medium Pen on paper
Brief Psychogeographic study of municipal areas. Textures, memory and the elusive feel of a space to create a sensory experience for the viewer.
Course Leader Matt Ward
Course BA Design

i33 / New Talent Refresh! Award / Bronze

Sponsored by The Coningsby Gallery /
Ben Aslett / Portraits

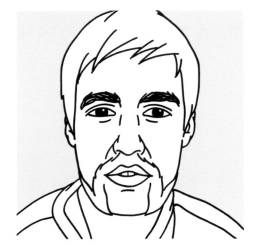

As a child I was dragged from pillar to post, but spent the majority of my life in the sunshine of Cyprus. I spent many a day occupied by beach activities, but constantly found myself absorbed in my own imagination. As a result of these experiences my horizons have been severely broadened, I have eclectic tastes and a passion for discovery, which has wormed its way into my illustration.

My recent work reflects my interest in nostalgic and photographic ephemera discovered in the numerous antique shops around the southwest. I enjoy creating peculiar and sometimes quite sinister looking characters and developing them within narrative forms.

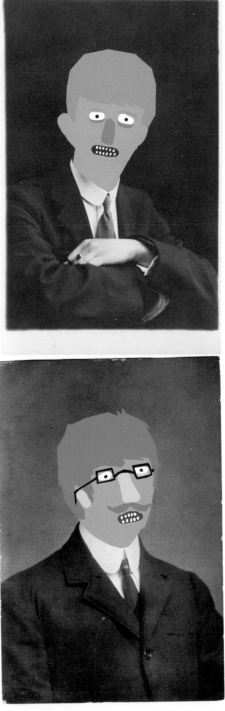

College University of Plymouth
Medium Collage and digital
Brief Experimental piece utilising a commonplace sense of disquiet.
Course Leader Ashley Potter
Course BA Illustration

Each entry is marked by the jury according
to how well the work fulfils the brief,
originality, and technical ability. Only
the highest scoring images are invited to
feature in the annual.

'One thing only I know and that is that I know nothing'

**Matthew Lloyd /
Socrates
College** Liverpool John Moores University
Medium Fine pen on paper
Brief My illustration reflects the
classic Greek philosopher Socrates, and
one of his famous quotes "One thing only
I know and that is that I know nothing".
Course Leader Mike O'Shaughnessy
Course Illustration

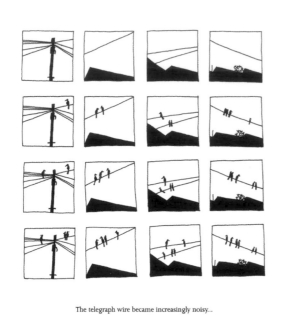

The telegraph wire became increasingly noisy...

Edgar plotted his escape.

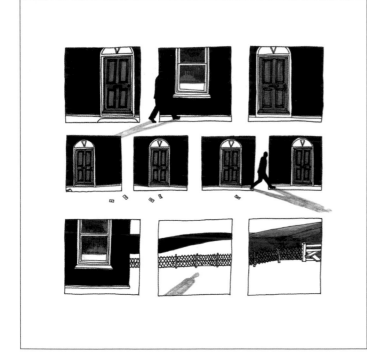

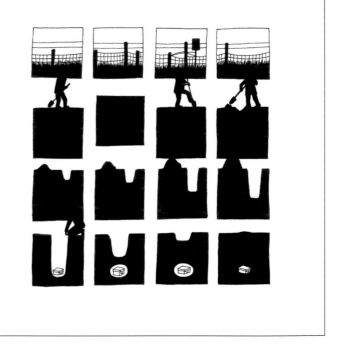

Chloë King
Liasing With Walrus
College Royal College of Art
Medium Pen and ink
Brief I was asked to use a Goya painting
as a starting point for a narrative
sequence. I combined this with notes
I make while travelling to develop a
graphic novella.
Course Leader Dan Fern
Course Communication Art and Design

Tony Lanchez
Jazz Brass
College Camberwell College of Arts
Medium Drawing and digital
Brief Portrait of Charlie Parker, Miles
Davies, Chet Baker and Lester Young.
Course Leader Janet Wooley
Course MA Illustration

Zara Picken
Crossed Wires
College University of the West of
England, Bristol
Medium Digital collage
Brief An editorial image for an article
about bilingual speakers and how language
signals to the brain can become confused.
Course Leader Gary Embury
Course BA (Hons) Illustration

Assisted Migration
College University of the West of
England, Bristol
Medium Digital collage
Brief An editorial image for an article
about entire species being relocated
to escape climates which are becoming
unsuitable for them.
Course Leader Gary Embury
Course BA (Hons) Illustration

Julia Bruderer
The Butcher Pig
College Central St Martins
Medium Monotype and acrylic on paper
Brief Commentary on animal cruelty.
Course Leader Andrew Foster / Gary Powell
Course MA Communication Design

The Bull
College Central St Martins
Medium Mono drawing with coloured
pencil on paper
Brief Man as half symbol, half animal.
Course Leader Andrew Foster / Gary Powell
Course MA Communication Design

go nuts with orange

give your friends a buzz

communication is branching out

Holly Sims /
Future Communication:
Giraffe / Squirrels / Bees
College University of Lincoln
Medium Gouache, pencil and Photoshop
Brief The brief was on the broad theme
of Future Communication for Orange.
Course Leader Howard Pemberton
Course BA (Hons) Illustration

Kate Aughey /
Stress Head
College Camberwell College
of Art, London
Medium Embroidered textile,
wire, feathers, found
objects
Brief To depict stress
including some of its
causes and side effects.
Course Leader Janet Woolley
Course MA Illustration

Deepa Vekaria /
A Conspiracy
College Central St. Martins
Medium Pen, ink, charcoal, acrylic paint,
block printing ink
Brief Explore the relationship between the
characters and the setting using stills
from Film Noir. To create a strong sense of
mood, atmosphere, suspense and loneliness.
Course Leader Andrew Foster
Course MA Communication Design: Illustration

James Green /
Harry, The Matador
College LJMU
Medium Mixed media collage
Brief Based on the innocent and vivid
imaginations of children. I asked my
5 year old neighbour if he knew what
bullfighting was. 'It's where the mista
has a red cape to fly away from the
bulls', he replied.
Course Leader Sandra Hiett
Course PGCE applied Art & Design

Douglas James Witter /
ZZZzzzzz / Cornflakes
College Southampton Solent University
Medium Mixed media
Brief I picked my brief on a book called
I lick my cheese and other notes from the
frontline of flat-sharing. I set myself
the task of reading the book and picking
the stories I found most interesting
and illustrating them with my own
interpretation.
Course Leader Peter Lloyd
Course Illustration

Iain Cox /
Remember All The Good Things
College University for the Creative
Arts, Maidstone
Medium Mixed media
Brief This piece reflects the
loneliness we all feel when beginning a
journey. The circular frames create a
sense of intimacy as well as distance,
as if we, the viewers, are spying on
these characters.
Course Leader Emily Mitchell,
Helga Steppan, Laura Carlin
Course Illustration

Tom Bown /
You've Got To Have Freedom /
No Shoes /
Bebop /
Nice Work If You Can Get It
College Southampton Solent University
Medium Screen-print
Brief The brief was to complete a series
of screen-prints inspired by 1960's and
modern New York City.
Course Leader Peter Lloyd
Course Illustration

›
Haruka Shinji /
Ocean Liner Toy Theatre
College Royal College Of Art
Medium Screen print
Brief Inspired by Goya's painting, this
paper theatre is designed to be built by
a customer.
Course Leader Dan Fern
Course Communication Art and Design

<

Rebecca Baker /
Come Into The Garden, Maud
College Southampton Solent University
Medium Coloured etching on Somerset
satin paper
Brief The etching illustrates Tennyson's
famous poem,'Come into the Garden, Maud'.
The central figure is Maud, staring out
at the viewer, gripping in her hand a
tiny bird which signifies her entrapment
and need for freedom. Maud is naked and
vulnerable, with elements of nature
covering her, referring to Eve from
the Bible.
Course Leader Peter Lloyd
Course Illustration

Dongyun Lee /
Hope
College School of Visual Arts
Medium Mixed media
Brief Dongyun Lee emphasizes contour and
line in his eight-foot-wide drawing Hope.
Populated with winged figures reminiscent
of Icarus, the artist offer viewers a
postmodern tableau from which they can
create their own narratives. Lee is a
recent alumnus from the MFA Illustration
as Visual Essay Department.
Course Leader Marshall Arisman
Course MFA Illustration as Visual Essay

Yann Brien /
Imaginary Friends
College Camberwell College of Arts
Medium Screen printing
Brief In this series, I drew a parallel between the delusions experienced by adults
suffering from an ever-expanding range of mental disorders, and the imaginary friends
very young children invent to keep them company when they feel sad, scared or lonely.
Course Leader Janet Woolley
Course MA Illustration

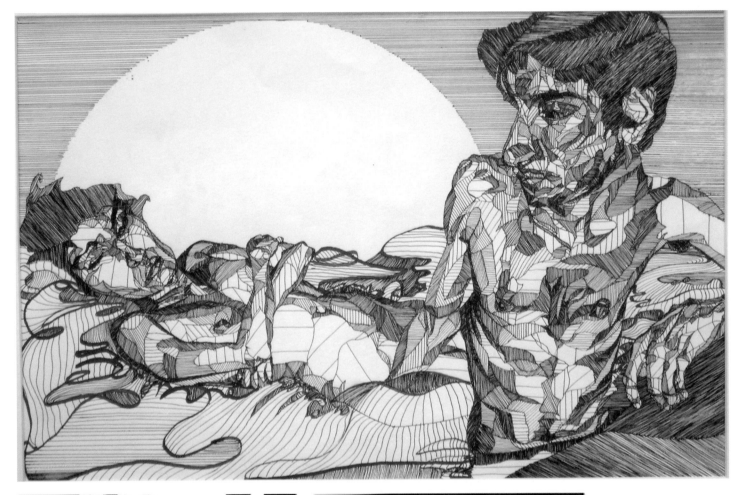

**Jamie Williams /
Felix Culpa**
College Huddersfield Univeristy
Medium Pen and ink on paper
Brief I re-interpreted John
Milton's Paradise Lost.
Humanizing the themes and
inserting contemporary
references. "Prefering hard
liberty to the easy yoke of
servile pomp".
Course Leader Robert Partridge
Course Fine Art: Drawing
& Painting

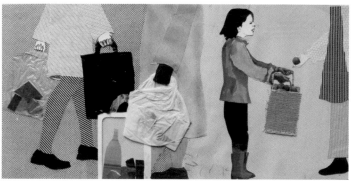

Laura Yates /
Jump On Your Bike /
Plastic Bags Are Rubbish /
Take The Train, Not The Plane
College Ecole de Communication Visuelle, Paris
Medium Recycled envelopes, plastic bags, collage
Brief Create a series of images to encourage
children and young people to get active on
climate change.
Course Leader Yann Thomas
Course Visual Communication

Space To Breathe
College Ecole de Communication Visuelle, Paris
Medium Pencil
Brief Create a poster on the theme of "The
City", for the "Graphisme dans la rue" festival,
Fontenay-sous-Bois, France.
Course Leader Vanessa Vérillon
Course Visual Communication

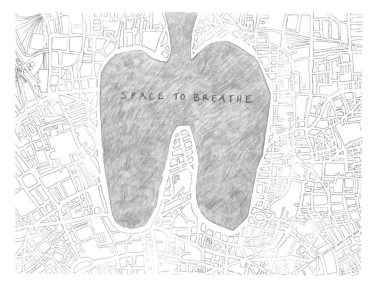

" THE [END] OF THE RACE IS JUST A TEMPORARY MARKER
WITHOUT MUCH SIGNIFICANCE.
IT'S THE SAME WITH OUR LIVES.
JUST BECAUSE THERE'S AN [END]
DOESN'T MEAN EXISTENCE HAS MEANING.
AN [END] POINT IS SIMPLY SET UP
AS A TEMPORARY MARKER,
OR PERHAPS AS AN INDIRECT METAPHOR
FOR THE FLEETING NATURE OF EXISTENCE. "

Simon Yewdall /
11:42:16 - Haruki Murakami
College Loughborough University School of
Art & Design
Medium Ink, acetate, sugar,
newspaper, computer
Brief Illustration inspired by the
journal entry made shortly after Haruki
Murakami finished the 100km ultramarathon
around Lake Saroma, Japan.
Course Leader Andy Selby
Course BA (Hons) Illustration

Caroline List
Head To Head
College Edinburgh College of Art
Medium Collage
Brief To illustrate a series of poems
by the writers Jane McKie and Andrew
Ferguson. Each poem and image is about
an individual character of a chess piece,
such as knight, bishop and king.
This book was published by Knucker
Press in 2008.
Course Leader Jonathan Gibbs
Course Mdes Illustration

Adriana Munoz /
Paulina
College Camberwell College of Arts
Medium 3D illustration
Brief From the found object -the ring-
drawing the possible owner.
Course Leader Janet Woolley
Course MA Illustration

Painful Shoes
College Camberwell College of Arts
Medium 3D illustration
Brief Story about a man who wears painful
shoes believing that when taking them off
he will find happiness.
Course Leader Janet Woolley
Course MA Illustration

Amandeep Singh
Weather Proverbs
College University of Hertfordshire
Medium Indian ink and Biro
Brief To create a self promotional piece
of work related to the weather. My idea
is directed towards the many weather
proverbs used in everyday society.
Course Leader Cathie Felstead
Course BA (Hons) Graphic Design
and Illustration

Identity
College University of Hertfordshire
Medium Indian ink, watercolour paint,
magazine and newspaper cutouts
Brief Produce an illustrated book about
yourself or someone else (but only if
you think you're far too uninteresting
as a subject).
Course Leader Cathie Felstead
Course BA (Hons) Graphic Design
and Illustration

Victoria Walker /
Imagine
College University of Sunderland
Medium Oil pastels, acrylic paints,
graphite pencil
Brief The idea was to produce a
children's picture book exploring
more philosophical themes, such as the
importance of imagination.
Course Leader Alison Barratt
Course MA Illustration and Design

Alex Bitskoff /
Rabbit's Dreams
College London College of Communication
Medium Gouache on paper, Photoshop
Brief The idea to illustrate my own
stories for the final major project in
LCC came to my mind straightaway. This
is one of few illustrations for the tale
about little rabbit who was looking for
his imaginary brother elephant.
Course Leader Karl Foster
Course Illustration

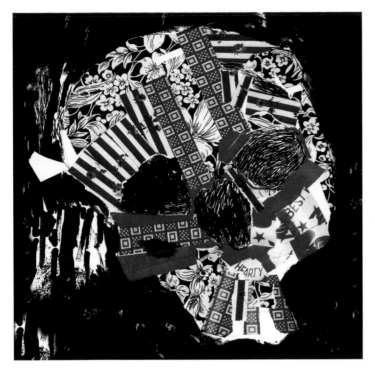

<
Rhys Bevan Jones /
Metaphors Of The Mind
College Kingston University
Medium Pen and ink, linocut/collograph
and digital
Brief I asked a number of people how
they visualised the mind. Some responded
through words and others through
drawings. I developed images based on
these ideas, and this is a selection
of the work. These were projected
in sequence on a large spherical
representation of the head.
Course Leader Geoff Grandfield
Course BA Illustration & Animation

Sammy Jones /
Dia De Muertos
College Southampton Solent University
Medium Collage, pen and ink
Brief The work is based on the infamous
Mexican festival entitled Dia De Muertos
(Day of the Dead). This is a time of
feasting and reunion when the dead are
believed to return to their family home
for one night, where they accept offerings
of special foods, flowers and clothes.
Course Leader Peter Lloyd
Course Illustration

Masako Kubo
The Giants Of St. Michael's Mount
College University College Falmouth
Medium Collage
Brief Children's book illustration for a
Cornish tale of the giants.
Course Leader Alan Male
Course BA (Hons) Illustration

Debbie Greenaway
Wanted Poster Of The Robber Bird
College University of Central Lancashire
Medium Screen print
Brief The Robber Bird Poster is part of an ongoing
self-initiated project. The aims are and were to
develop my story generating ideas by the fun creation
of narrative illustrations with a strong emphasis on
character design and the use of typography.
Course Leader Steve Wilkin
Course Illustration

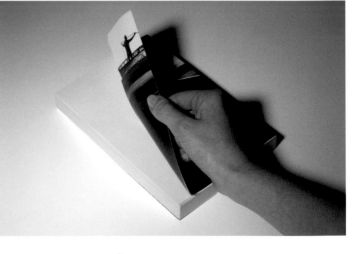

Lydia Fee /
The Old Man And The Sea
College Loughborough University
Medium Mixed media
Brief This cover questions theories about Hemingway's use of Christian symbolism and metaphor. The design is supported by a format that both conceals and reveals, reflecting the debate that surrounds this.
Course Leader Andy Selby
Course BA (Hons) Illustration

>
Casper" Ho /
Detail Project
College Central Saint Martins College Of Art And Design
Medium Pencil, Photoshop printed on paper & tracing paper
Brief Re-illustrate old project for portfolio in 2007.
Course Leader Howard Tangye
Course BA (Hons) Fashion Design: Womenswear

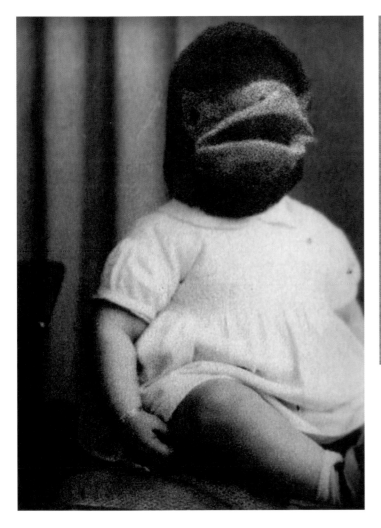

Poop in Soupers:
University of Plymouth Students
UoP Window
Paticipating students: Jess Douglas,
Chloe Ehninger, Jack Teagle, Jack
Gingold, Donya Todd, Clare Owen, Ben
Aslett, Philip Ha, Laura Kingdon
College University of Plymouth
Medium Acrylic, marker pen
Brief A collaborative piece by nine
students to advertise the degree show,
open days and the illustration department
to the city. To be executed in 2 days.
Course Leader Ashley Potter
Course BA Illustration

Steph Walker /
Levinsky Building
College University of Plymouth
Medium Acrylic, pencil and digital
Brief Location study "A sense of
place" based around the University's
new architecture.
Course Leader Ashley Potter
Course BA Illustration

Nick Cran /
Family Album
College University of Plymouth
Medium Digital collage
Brief To explore the presence of disquiet
amongst the family as epitomised by the
"one for sorrow" nursery rhyme.
Course Leader Ashley Potter
Course BA Illustration

Oliver Butcher /
Hungry
College University of Plymouth
Medium Paint, Tippex and crayon
Brief A wordless narrative following
a character who is consumed with a
perpetual hunger. The project theme
was "Food".
Course Leader Ashley Potter
Course BA Illustration

Stephen Daoud /
Bear Reaches A Tree
College University of Plymouth
Medium Pen and ink, digital
Brief A wordless narrative which explores
the desire to be something that you're
not. The bear wants to be a bird and fly.
Course Leader Ashley Potter
Course BA Illustration

<
Ciaran McFadden /
Unsolved Case 4
College University of Plymouth
Medium Acrylic and digital
Brief To combine skills of rendering with
a sense of oddness and disquiet.
Course Leader Ashley Potter
Course BA Illustration

Mark Smith /
The Big Squeeze
College University of Plymouth
Medium Scanned drawings and Photoshop
Brief For an article I saw in the
Guardian outlining the country's oncoming
economic difficulties.
Course Leader Ashley Potter
Course BA Illustration

Tourist
College University of Plymouth
Medium Ink and Photoshop
Brief An open brief to produce a
series of something. I chose to make
a concertina book that illustrates a
fictional moment in time.
Course Leader Ashley Potter
Course BA (Hons) Design: Illustration

Liz Kay /
I'm A Woman
College University of Lincoln
Medium Acrylic, watercolour and collage
Brief Produce a series of images based
on the 1963 song 'I'm a woman' sung by
Peggy Lee.
Course Leader Howard Pemberton
Course Illustration

Kaeleigh Beddoe /
Patchwork Monkey
College University of Plymouth
Medium Watercolour, gouache and colour pencil
Brief For a calendar based on the natural history
section of Royal Albert Memorial Museum, Exeter.
Course Leader Ashley Potter
Course BA Illustration

<

Ellie Foreman-Peck /
The Taming Of The Lion
College University of the West of England
Medium Pen, pencil and Photoshop
Brief Design an Invite for the UWE
Illustration degree show at the
Conningsby gallery, London.
Course Leader Chris Hill
Course BA (Hons) Illustration

Laura Meredith /
Dead For A Week
College University of Portsmouth
Medium Polymer clay, acrylic, fabric,
mixed materials
Brief Degree work exploring the subject
of unclaimed bodies, particularly
focusing on the elderly who are isolated
within the community and may die
unnoticed and unmourned.
Course Leader Bob Wright
Course Illustration

Meng-Chia Lai /
Red String
College Royal College of Art
Medium Acrylic ink on paper
Brief An old Chinese myth says, there
is an invisible red string tied around
your little finger since you were born.
It connects to the little finger of your
love for life. This book is based on
this myth and also inspired by the love
stories I have heard from my friends.
Course Leader Dan Fern
Course Communication Art & Design

Pilipala
College Royal College of Art
Medium Gouache on paper
Brief Pilipala is the sound of rainning
in Mandarin. In this work, I created the
images through my memories, imagination
and expression inspired by the
interactions with others and the nature.
In this book, a lot of thoughts, and
emotions coming down like "Pilipala."
Course Leader Dan Fern
Course Communication Art & Design

Jonathan Lam /
Romance, Revenge, Revolution
College Middlesex University
Medium Drawing with digital manipulation
Brief A poster to promote the opera to a new audience who might previously have thought it was for elites.
Course Leader Nancy Slonims
Course BA (Hons) Illustration

Cristian Ortiz /
Boy And Bear (With Hair)
College Middlesex University
Medium Pen drawing with digital colour
Brief A page from my graphic novel, Boy and Bear, printed in an edition of fifty.
Course Leader Nancy Slonims
Course BA (Hons) Illustration

Matthew Frame /
This Is Cactus Land
College Middlesex University
Medium Ink drawing
Brief One of a sequence of images illustrating The Wasteland, the modernist poem by T. S. Eliot.
Course Leader Nancy Slonims
Course BA (Hons) Illustration

Alice Mazzilli /
Tau Zero
College Middlesex University
Medium Collage and letterpress
Brief A book cover design for Poul Anderson's novel Tau Zero, which explores themes of accelerating time.
Course Leader Nancy Slonims
Course BA (Hons) Illustration

This is cactus land

Fifty men and women set out in the twenty -third century from Earth aboard an interstellar craft to travel to a planet some thirty light-years away.
The ship will approach the speed of light and so (as Einstein predicted) subjective time on board will slow and so the jurney of several decades will be of much shorter duration for the crew.
But the ship's deceleration system is irreparably damaged when it hits a clowd of interstellar dust and accelleration continues toward light speed tau zero.
Soon the ship is speeding through galaxies and eons are passing on board the ship in a blink of an eye...

POUL ANDERSON

TAU ZERO

TAU ZERO

POUL ANDERSON

<

Joanna Wilson /
My Father
College Middlesex University
Medium Lino cut
Brief A linocut of my father. This is one of a series of images
exploring lino as a medium for portraits in an editorial context.
Course Leader Nancy Slonims
Course BA (Hons) Illustration

Gulls
College Middlesex University
Medium Lino cut
Brief To explore the expressive qualities of traditional
linocutting, within the context of seaside reportage.
Course Leader Nancy Slonims
Course BA (Hons) Illustration

Tara Cloak /
Viva!
College Central St Martins
Medium Copper plate etching
Brief To represent the typical Mexican
Independence day fiesta when the bells
are rung in the streets and the crowds
shout 'Viva!'.
Course Leader Ann Course
Course BA (Hons) GraDes

i33 / About the AOI

The Association of Illustrators was established in 1973 to advance and protect illustrators' rights and is a non-profit making trade association dedicated to its members' professional interests and the promotion of contemporary illustration. As the only body to represent illustrators and campaign for their rights in the UK, the AOI has successfully increased the standing of illustration as a profession and improved the commercial and ethical conditions of employment for illustrators. On behalf of its members and with their continued support, the AOI can achieve goals that it would be difficult or impossible for creators to attempt alone.

A voice for illustration
The AOI provides a voice for professional illustrators and by weight of numbers and expertise is able to work at enforcing the rights of freelance illustrators at every stage of their careers. AOI liaises with national and international organisations, art buyers, agents and illustrators over industry problems and campaigns against unfair contracts and terms of trade.

Campaigning and Net-working
The AOI is responsible for establishing the right for illustrators to retain ownership of their artwork and helped to establish the secondary rights arm of the Designers and Artists Copyright Society (DACS), the UK visual arts licensing society. In addition, it lobbies parliament for better legislation for illustrators though the British Copyright Council (BCC) and the Creators Rights Alliance (CRA). The AOI is also a founder member of the European Illustrators Forum (EIF) a network of 20 member associations in Europe established to exchange information, co-ordinate exhibitions and conferences and create a stronger force for illustrators within Europe and the European Commission.

Pro-Action: Illustration Campaign and Liaison Group
The Pro-Action committee was established by the AOI and the Society of Artists Agents to deal with the problems facing illustrators in today's market place. The groups aims are to tackle fee erosion, increasingly detrimental contract terms from clients and issues that may arise between illustrators and their representatives. These factors have increasingly become a negative force effecting creators of visual material working in the commercial communications arena over the last 25 years.
For further information please visit pro-action.org.uk

Information and Support Services
AOI continues to improve services to its members, and ensures they are kept up to date with relevant industry information. Members of the AOI not only sustain campaigning and networking to improve working conditions for all, they benefit personally from AOI services.

Members stay informed with our wide range of events and seminars. Varoom magazine, UP info poster and the monthly Despatch newsletter keep members up to date with events, practice and developments in the industry. Members receive up to 50% off our topical range of events and forums, themes ranging from children's books, to self-promotion, business planning and up-to-the-minute industry debates.

Resources to help illustrators succeed
Members receive large discounts on essential publications, including the Images annual, The Illustrator's Guide to Law and Business Practice, The Illustrator's Guide to Success and our range of targeted directory listings of illustration commissioners. Members of the AOI receive discounts in art shops around the country.

Resources to help commissioners succeed
The AOI's Guide to Commissioning Illustration saves time and money by guiding commissioners safely through the pitfalls of the commissioning process. Commissioners receive Images, the only jury-selected source book in the UK, free of charge. Our online portfolios at AOIportfolios.com give commissioners looking for the perfect artist for their projects access to more than 8000 classified images and the creator's contact details in a click.

Essential professional and business advice
Members have access to a free dedicated hotline for legal, ethical and pricing advice, discounted consultations with our pool of industry specialists including business advisors, a chartered accountant and a portfolio consultant.

Promotion
Members can receive substantial discounts on the AOI's online portfolios at AOIportfolios.com and our Images competition and exhibition, showcasing the best of British contemporary illustration. The annual is despatched to over 4000 prominent commissioners of illustration in the UK and overseas. All information on Images can be found at AOIimages.com

Inspiration
Talks with leading illustrators, industry debates and discounted entry to competitions and exhibitions. Members receive a free subscription to Varoom magazine - a sumptuous celebration of 'made' images. It features interviews with leading illustrators and image-makers as well as in-depth articles on different aspects and themes of contemporary illustration. It's stimulating line-up of interviews, profiles, history and polemic make Varoom essential reading for everyone interested in visual communication. See more at varoom-mag.com

Contact
To request further information or a membership application form please telephone +44 (0)20 7613 4328 or email info@theaoi.com

Website
Visit the AOI's website at theAOI.com for details of the Association's activities, details of forthcoming events and online tickets, listings and reviews, the AOI's history, and to purchase publications or view online portfolios.

The illustrator's guide to success

Published by the AOI, the Guide to Success is the most comprehensive and in-depth guide to illustration as a professional career – from the organisation that knows! Established illustrators, agents, clients and a range of other professionals have contributed to the beautifully illustrated, up to date publication. Each area of the profession including portfolio presentation, self-promotion, agents and copyright issues are looked at in detail. The wealth of information in the Guide to Success makes it absolutely indispensable to the newcomer and also has much to offer the more experienced illustrator.

The illustrator's guide to law and business practice

Updated, expanded and redesigned with contemporary illustrations this comprehensive guide covers all aspects of the law affecting illustrators. It contains recommended terms and conditions, advice on calculating fees, how to write a licence agreement and protect yourself against exploitative practices.

The handbook has been written by Simon Stern, a renowned expert on illustration and the law, and is the result of many years of research. It has been approved by intellectual property experts, law firm Finers Stephens Innocent.

Report on illustration fees and standards of pricing

This informative report was revised in April 2007 with the latest information from an online survey, new AOI data from the last two years and invaluable contributions from agents, art buyers and selected working professionals.

Properly researched costing and pricing st ructures is a central plank in maintaining business viability, and illustrators should consider the true cost of their services when determining rates. AOI believes this report will create awareness of the importance of carefully considered pricing for both illustrators and commissioners.

Client directories

AOI produce three essential directories. The Publishing Directory lists circa 170, and the Editorial Directory more than 300 illustration clients with full contact details; the Advertising Directory holds details of over 150 advertising agencies who commission illustration – providing an invaluable source of information for all practitioners. Each directory includes notes of what kind of illustration is published by the client and we update and add contact details to each list every year. CD ROMs are also supplied with addresses and pre-formatted labels for printing.

Varoom

Varoom is devoted to exploring the world of illustration and image-making. The magazine looks at practitioners from around the world who are making significant contributions to the constantly evolving art of illustration, on both a commercial and culturally significant level. Varoom provides writers, commentators and illustrators with a platform from which to take a critical yet accessible look at trends and developments in the illustrated image.

Published three times a year. 84 pages, ISSN 1750-483X, available in specialist bookshops in the UK, Europe, USA and Canada, free to members.

The Varoom website has information on current and back issues, and features web-only content, reviews, articles ad listings. varoom-mag.com

To order publications online visit the AOI's online shop at theAOI.com
To subscribe to Varoom go to varoom-mag.com
For further information please contact the Association of Illustrators on
+44 (0)20 7613 4328
or email info@theaoi.com

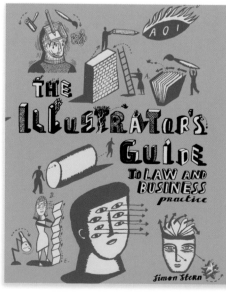

Up poster

Published quarterly, UP is a collectible
item featuring a unique image each issue.
UP not only looks great on your wall it
also keeps you up to date with AOI news
and events, reports on important industry
developments and recommends exhibitions that
could inspire you.

Despatch email newsletter

Despatch, published monthly, brings you
the latest industry news, AOI events
information, campaigns, initiatives and
listings of relevant exhibitions and
publications. To subscribe, visit the News
section on the AOI website.

theAOI.com

Illustration resources for commissioners
and practitioners.

Visit the website for details on
AOI membership and the Association's
activities, including Despatch newsletters
and articles from our previous membership
magazine - The Journal, details of
forthcoming events and campaigns, the AOI's
history, news and reviews, and to purchase
publications and tickets.

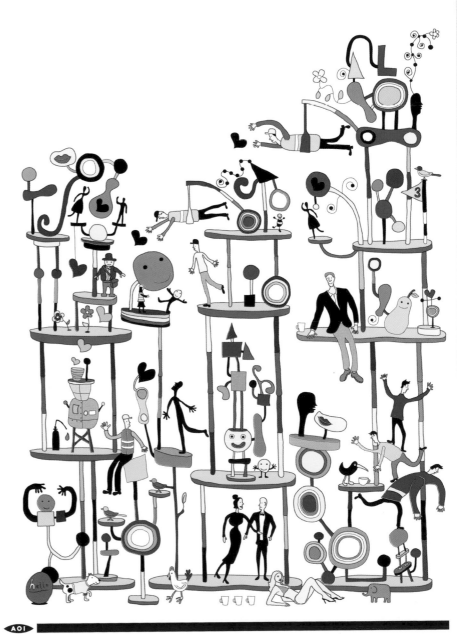

The AOI would like to thank all members of the jury for applying their expertise to the difficult task of selecting the best of all the entries now published in this book. As always, to Sabine Reimer for her efficiency and cheerful dedication during the production of Images 33.

Special thanks go to Images 33 art director, Adrian Shaughnessy, for the bold new cover and design, and to Simon Sharville for his creative involvement during the design process. Also to Hannah Buck for creating the portraits throughout the annual.

Kenneth Andersson, whose image "Big Dog" was used for the promotion of the call for entries for Images 33.

Images 33 could not have been organised without the help of our dedicated casual staff and volunteers and we are very grateful for their invaluable assistance, especially Anna Steinberg and Simon Daw.

Last but not least, we are grateful for the support of the many organisations and individuals who contribute to the success of the Images exhibition and annual by submitting their work for others to judge.

arena

THE ART MARKET
illustration agency

CIA

the coningsby gallery

début art

eastwing

FITCH

FORTUNE ST

theguardian

GULLANE
CHILDREN'S BOOKS

Illustration

KINDRED

meadowside
CHILDREN'S BOOKS

ORCHARD BOOKS

Portobello
BOOKS

Global

Property
Week.

RANDOM HOUSE CHILDREN'S BOOKS

THE ARTWORKS

CUT OFF

Shine *your* light

with AOIportfolios.com

The illustration resource for art-buyers and commissioners has been developed by the Association of Illustrators to promote contemporary illustration to the creative industries

Association of illustrators

Illustration by Delphine Lebourgeois

An award winning

Go to varoom-mag.com

Back issues still available £8
03, 05, 06, 07, 08, 09

Current issue £12

collection

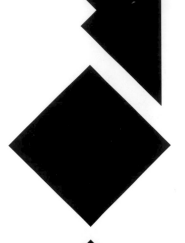
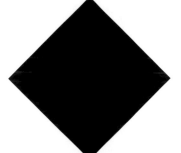

2009
issue 06, 07 and 08
Award of Typographic Excellence NYC
Type Directors Club

issue 05, 06, 07
STEP Design 100 Annual

2008
issue 05 cover
Communication Arts Design Annual

Short-listed for the Design Museum's
Designs of the Year Awards

2007
Selected for The Creative Review Annual
Selected for D&AD Annual
Short-listed for the Design Week Awards

Illustrated lettering edition.

the journal of illustration and made images

05

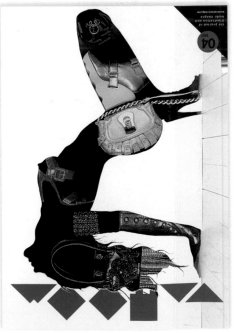

the journal of illustration and made images

04